MILLENNIAL POETRY

Dr Olalekan Fagbola
MILLENNIAL POETRY

Published by Spines
ISBN: 979-8-89569-086-4

MILLENNIAL POETRY
A Unique Book of Modern Poetry with Footnotes

Dr Olalekan Fagbola

I am grateful to the all-powerful divine force behind the creation of all things, both living and non-living, for bringing me into existence as a part of this universe. I also extend my thanks to my parents Mrs S. A and Chief B. A Fagbola, whose combined DNA provided the path to the safe conduit through which I entered this mysterious world. My brother Adebisi Fagbola's foresight ensured that I experienced all the corners of primary and secondary schools. Lastly, I owe special thanks to my immediate family members wife Marilyn and children Bibitayo and Olatunji whose support has made this publication possible.

INTRODUCTION

Millennial Poetry emerged from a quest for a title that captures contemporary life. In the days of old poetic language often proved overly intricate. When I attended secondary school, numerous students were deterred from literature due to their aversion to the complexities of poetry. A particularly daunting aspect was the unseen prose section in the West African School Certificate Examinations, which posed a significant challenge to many literature students. After reviewing past question papers and realizing the difficulty of the compulsory unseen poem and unseen prose questions, many students opted to remove literature from their list of subjects for the exit examinations.

The language of Millennial or Modern Poetry is not strictly bound by the rules and thematic application, rhythms, and idioms written and spoken in traditional poetry. The experience of people in the 20th century is much different from those of the old era. Readers and lovers of poetry are drawn to poems with less complexity compared to difficult-to-understand verses of the years of yore.

In today's world, opportunities abound that were unheard of in the past. We are fortunate to seamlessly blend imagination and reality in moments of reflection, creating literary works that attract readership. Social media platforms such as Facebook, Instagram, WhatsApp, Telegram, and others unite people, facilitating the sharing of pictures, exchange of business ideas, pursuit of education, and more. These virtual interactions are integral to inspiring creative ideas.

As a guitar and harmonica player, I have veered into the arena penning lyrics and writing songs. Therefore, a few poems that surface in this book have a lyrical structure. I have also indulged myself a little in musing on various issues discussed at social gatherings, traveling experiences, and observing human behaviour.

No one mode of communication can adequately express our feelings on different issues, our experiences in many areas, and our encounters with certain people. Certain things are better written than vocalized and what is for one-on-one dialogue may not be suitable for communal briefing. The poems in sections one and two are accompanied by short prose of footnotes to highlight the embedded messages they carry.

About the Book

Millennial Poetry is a curated anthology that explores the vast landscape of love life, people and events, village life, friends and colleagues, quest for peace, praise poems and miscellaneous topics through the delicate art of poetry. This collection is a tribute to the myriad facets of existence, divided into thematic sections that offer readers a rich medley of emotions and reflections. From the tender whispers of love to the solemn quest for peace, this book is designed to resonate with anyone who has ever pondered the complexities of life in its various facets of mystery.

The Layouts contain Seven Sections

Love Poems: This section makes incursion into many dimensions of love, capturing its beauty, pain, and transformative power. The poems range from passionate declarations and wishful longing to the serene comforts of companionship. Each of the 22 poems in the section has been crafted to evoke the intimate and profound nature of romantic relationships thus offering readers a glimpse into the myriad ways love shapes our lives.

People and Events: The 13 poems here focus on the individuals and events that leave an indelible mark on the author. Through vivid imagery and poignant reflections, this section brings to life the stories and events that shape personal narratives.

Village Life: In the village setting were written 4 poems that recall the background in which the author spent part of his early life, where his father's farm estate was one of the largest in the area. Farming is one of the oldest occupations. In the Abrahamic religions—Judaism, Christianity, and Islam—the holy books indicate that the first man and woman lived in a garden. Although no mention was made of their specific occupation, their descendants starting from Cain and Abel were engaged in rural farming and animal husbandry moving from place to place as itinerant shepherds.

Friends and Colleagues: The sacred bonds of friendship and the dynamics of professional relationships are explored in this section. The 23 poems in this section honor the loyalty, camaraderie, and shared experiences that characterize these connections. Whether celebrating the joy of a lifelong friend or the respect between colleagues, these verses highlight the importance of human connection in both personal and professional spheres.

Quest for Peace: The author wades into his involvement in peace advocacy in a meditative exploration of the longing for tranquillity in a tumultuous world. The 3 poems in this section address regional wars, appeal for global peace, societal harmony, and the universal desire for a world free from conflict. Through introspective verses and calls for unity, this section reflects on the challenges and aspirations associated with achieving lasting peace.

Miscellaneous Topics: Consisting of 8 poems, this eclectic section offers a diverse range of subjects, from whimsical musings to profound observations on everyday life. It serves as a creative playground where the poet's imagination can roam free, touching on everything from nature's wonders to philosophical ponderings. This variety ensures that readers encounter unexpected delights and thought-provoking insights.

Praise Poems: As the name suggests, the focus of the 39 poems here is on celebrating excellence and recognizing the exceptional qualities of individuals, places, and concepts. These poems are dedicated to honoring achievements, virtues, and the beauty found in both the extraordinary and the commonplace. Through uplifting and appreciative language, this section serves as a reminder of the good that exists in the world.

Millennial Poetry is an exploration of the human condition through the lens of poetic expression. Each section invites readers to reflect, connect, and find solace in the shared experiences that unite and sadly divide human beings. Whether you seek the comfort of love, or the serenity of peace, this anthology offers a poetic journey through the diverse facets of life.

CONTENTS

Section Three

Section Four

SECTION ONE

LOVE POEMS

Torn Between Two

He resides in my mind, you in my heart reside always
Often, I see you, he occupies my thoughts all the time
Strange as it may sound, uncertain where my passion lies
Genuine care and love, equally for you both I have.

You differ from him in behavior and personality,
You are outgoing and friendly, he is reclusive,
You are tall and slender, he is short and stout,
You drink socially and occasionally, he is teetotal.

I am perplexed to fall for two people who admire me,
So distinct in every way indescribable,
Yet, I want you both just as you are.
I do desire and don't I deserve to experience both worlds fully?

Blessed or guilty, my emotions swirl within and around.
Caught in the web of matters of the heart seeking resolution,
The weave of attraction draws me to masculinity and sensuality
Occasioned by my taste for men of refined standards.

A gainfully employed young, beautiful, and successful career woman finds herself torn between two men who couldn't be more different in every aspect of their lives in vital statistics, personalities, and behaviour patterns. Standing at a crossroads, she wrestles with her weird choices, unable to justify her unconventional decision to keep both and possibly marry them if they agree to her wishful request.

Cleverly and courageously, she decides to handle the situation unusually. She penned a heartfelt poem to express her feelings sent to the two men by WhatsApp, laying bare her soul in a bold take-it-or-leave-it approach. Different emotions of both guys are poetically revealed through the verses of the poem below titled 'I Accept My Fate' and 'Obsession.'

I Accept My Fate and Reality

Emotions may be easy to display, though not always.
Certain types of feelings are difficult to control or express.
More often than not, people have reasons for their choices.
Being attracted to someone has pull and push factors.

The hallmark of appeal is when we are
Inexplicably drawn to an individual;
We like them and want to be around them.

Desperately as we may want to share
The same space with someone,
Tried hard as we may wish and want
To have them look our way romantically,
Seriously as we may need them,
To be part of our life journey,
Things that are practically beyond
Our range of attainment,
Are better left alone to preserve sanity
And for normalcy restoration.
So, I accept my fate and reality,
When my lover doesn't share his love with me alone.

The man declines the proposition rather than becoming entangled in a love triangle web. This serves as a lesson to those who view being in love with a particular person as a make-or-break affair. The truth and reality are that, when you lose a lover to someone else, one of two outcomes is likely to follow, typically. You may find someone better or worse than the one you willingly let go or lose circumstantially but certainly, never someone the same as him or her. It is incumbent on you to secure a better bargain.

Obsession

How I struggle to focus; scattered are my thoughts,
All because of you, the captor of my mind.
Every corner, every space of me you fill,
And got me folded in your tightened grip.

It would help if you understood that deep in my core,
Is where you are, being the one I long for.
Cherished are you by me in every second,
Hoping that you stay forever by me and for me.

Faithfully by your side stay I will,
In all and every conceivable reality.
We are meant to be this way for long,
For ours are two wild but free souls bound.

Consumed I am in thought by your essence,
Lust, passion, and fantasy got me lost in obsession.
Unstoppably falling for you, sanely as things get serious
How I wish you get sanely serious with me.

———

Unlike the first man who accepts his fate and moves on, the second man pleads his case, striving to prove he deserves her love and is unwilling to give up. Does he love her more than the first man does? That remains unclear, but the woman herself may ultimately determine whose love holds greater weight based on their actions and how they make her feel.

Genius Offspring for Us

Constantly thinking of you gives me immense pleasure.
The anticipation of love reciprocity gives me tremendous joy.
Seeing you around most of the weekdays makes me happy.
The thought of you and I being together gets me excited.
But then, I can't see enough of you as I would like to.
I pinch myself to be sure I'm consciously feeling the way I feel.
I am not obsessed; it is your persona that blows off my mind.
I am not weird; it is your graceful poise that gets me fascinated.

Soft on the eyes, yours is the natural beauty of an uncommon kind.
Sexy and confident, your hairstyle appreciably sets you apart.
It is delightful to see you walk elegantly and stylishly.
Your imposing figure with smooth skin commands my attention.
Your illuminating eyes can search me for truthfulness.
Straight legs like poles, please boogie with me on the dance floor.
Hold me with your soft hands in a demonstrated sign of affection.
Face to face, belly to belly, torso to torso, let's rock and roll.

Your winsome smiles warm my heart and lift my spirit.
Classy customized dress sprinkled with designer cologne.
Everything about you makes me susceptible to feminine lure.
I can do with your trademark infectious laughter to ginger me up.
The admixture of your soft and loud sweet voice is good for me.
A multi-career woman and a multitalented man are
complimentary.
Things are all the better, our career paths cross in the healthcare
field.
We should be a couple and bring forth genius offspring.

---

*The poem was inspired by a friend whose conversation with his girlfriend
I overheard while we were chilling out in a restaurant. They both work in
the same rarefied career field, pursued by a select few around the world.
Reflecting on their unique profession, his thoughts wandered to the
prospect of their future marriage, envisioning it as potentially blessed
with exceptionally gifted children who could be geniuses.*

Love Affirmation

Into my eyes, you should look.
Written there is love affirmation.
All around my head, body, and limbs,
Your affection is verily wrapped,
Much like a tight-fitting dress
That accentuates the body curves.

Into the chambers of my heart,
Your love is poured continuously.
They are filled up and the love overflows.
The desire to have you is a constant,
In an unbalanced mathematics equation
That is difficult to solve by any formula.

Being involved with someone with insecurity issues can put a strain on the relationship. One has to constantly reassure the insecure party. Bigger problems would surface as time goes on. Jealousy, accusation, doubt, and lack of trust are likely to bedevil the union. Depending on the individuals involved, counseling and therapy are suggested to boost confidence.

However, one must weigh whether to stay in or leave the relationship, considering the compatibility of attributes. This situation reminds me of a couple who lived next door. The husband was monitored almost daily by his wife, who sent him endless messages at work. Despite being a devoted husband, he had to provide his work schedule for the week to her. Eventually, he sought advice from a psychologist who diagnosed her with low self-esteem, insecurity, and trust issues afflicting his wife.

Consequently, they resorted to renewing their wedding vows annually to illustrate their commitment to overcoming these longstanding challenge issues together.

All I Have for You is Love

All the while, I have been emotionally connected to you.
From being a random admirer to an avowed, devoted lover,
You are kindly required to bless me with your love.
All I have and feel for you is unconditional love.

The Cupid's arrow I fired at you from a distance
Rebounded, pierced my heart, and created a spot in it.
The effect of it makes me weak for you in earnest.
Let my wish to have you crystallize into reality.

Strong is your presence with me always.
I crave to hold you close so we cuddle endlessly,
That I yearn for a long, sensuous embrace,
Chest to chest, to feeling each other's heartbeat forever.

Certainly, it is not uncommon to find oneself in a less than ideal situation where love is unrequited by longing for someone who remains unaware of the emotional bond with them. This scenario frequently unfolds in the realm obsession for celebrities. People often become infatuated with entertainer like movie stars, sports idols, politicians, or business magnates and highly accomplished individuals. In higher institutions, students become emotionally attached to lecturers consciously and or otherwise. Some individuals become fixated on these figures to an unhealthy degree that can lead to behavior patterns like stalking or even physical harming the ones that are admired. Tragically, fatal attractions have resulted from such unattainable desires, leaving secret admirers with dreams never to be realized.

What Love Does

Happiness in love some find while endurance of pain is others' lot.
Some inflict wounds, while others heal the wounds of love.
Some harm for love, while others rehabilitate the harmed.
Some destroy, while others save lives for love.

True love grows when nurtured and handled with care.
It flourishes in an environment of mutual regard and respect.
It withers and dies in a toxic atmosphere fueled by jealousy.
It thrives when healthy individuals engage in it.

Love is often the reason many people don't achieve great success.
Love is also the cause of emotional turmoil for many.
Love respects boundaries but itself knows no bounds.
It is what both the young and the old yearn to give and receive.

Without an iota of doubt, love enriches the lives of millions worldwide although a significant portion of the global population does not experience its positive effects. One could argue that a considerable percentage of human challenges stem from romantic and even platonic relationships. For every seven couples who happily navigate friendship and love, there are often three troubled relationships at various stages. Not all marriages are filled with blissful stories; many careers have been paused to give priority to love.

While some celebrate successful relationships and partnerships, others lament endless tales of hardship brought about by being involved in a relationship. Various factors can erode the attractiveness of a partner in a marriage or girlfriend/boyfriend relationship. Among them are financial demands, unrealistic expectations, personality changes, and physical transformations which often disrupt relationship dynamics, leading to infidelity, incompatibility, separation, or outright divorce. The verses in the poem titled "Love is Not a Good Thing" should not be dismissed as mere poetic exercise; they reflect profound truths about the complexities of love in society among the rich or poor.

Love Is Not a Good Thing

There is no universally accepted definition.
It defies consensus of opinions,
I t is felt and experienced almost the same way
By the gullible who believe in it irrationally.
It intoxicates much like vodka,
Concentrated palm wine,
Nasty brew with devastating effects,
Enslaver of the well-intentioned.

It is worth it when mutually experienced.
The best emotional investment though,
For those who carelessly mutually
Embark on the terrible emotional journey
That makes the sane and sober run mad,
As unmeasurable as unquantifiable.
It burns like fire but soothes like nice music,
Scorching like the sun but cooling like menthol.

Some are happy in love, others endure the pain of a relationship.
Some inflict wounds while others heal the wounds for love.
Some maim for love while others rehabilitate the maimed.
Some kill while others save life for love's sake.
It grows if it is nurtured and handled with care.
It blossoms in an environment of regard and respect.
It withers and dies in a toxic milieu driven by jealousy.
It is healthy when healthy people dabble in it.
It respects boundaries but has no boundaries.
It is what the old and young yearn to give and get.

Valuable like gold but useless like a dumbass.
Sacred as a religious icon but profane as cuss words.
They say you gain many things when in love,
And lose a lot when you find no one to love.
You're apprehensive to fall, scared silly to fall out,
In the crossroads of indecision and confusion.
It could be I did but did not know I ever did.
Love is not a good thing but loving is good.

Stolen Love

She loves him but is not in love with him!
Shock-like delivered; genuinely felt and absorbed,
He cannot hide his emotional pain and unhappiness
Over the unfortunate act of unfaithfulness
An act committed by the one he loves and trusts.

In his world, she has love, care and consideration.
Unfortunately, however, passion and compassion
Swept her feet off the ground into the air
In a dance of promiscuity, immediate gratification
To satisfy overwhelming sexual desire.
But no love involved, only infatuation.

She deluded herself with righteous indignation
a misinterpretation of being loved and cherished
Ba y a 'bumper and dumper' of lecherous man.
Given day-dreaming, the theoretical speculation
A far cry from the practical outcome when the chips are down.
No one loves a renegade, but only to be lied to,
Fucked with and hissed at again and again.

The trilogy of Stolen Love, Stolen Kiss, and Stolen Sex, detailed across the following two pages, shares a common theme briefly explained in the footnote on Stolen Sex. Stolen Love initiates Stolen Kiss, which in turn progresses to Stolen Sex, illustrating a sequence where each step serves as a precursor to the next.

Stolen Kiss

They are telling tales of burning desires,
Intense kisses for amorous individuals.
He planted them firmly and possessively,
On her cheeks and succulent lips,
Spread by makeup to areas unintended,
To seal a deal of yearning and wanting.

As they lovingly embrace each other,
Whispering sweet words of endearment,
He caresses her from the earlobes to the chin,
And gently massages every delineated curve.
The breasts are not spared his soft touches,
That is beginning to bring out the best in her.

They passionately smooch and wildly cuddle,
With her arms longingly encircling his neck,
Her rotund butts were firmly cupped by his palms.
A pair of searching eyes probing his body.

Impatient to get behind closed doors,
They disappear from their rendezvous.
Nightfall seems so eternal, in coming.
Two bodies entwine and four legs interlock.
They are talking but the sounds are muffled,
Fully aroused to the point of no return.
Their breathing is now heavy and deep,
In the expected climax of stolen kisses.

The culmination of Stolen Kiss is fully narrated in Stolen Sex but in a paraphrased form here. Enjoy following the story as it unfolds sequentially on the next page.

Stolen Sex

Pretty face, sexy body, all nature's gifts.
Beautiful to look at but hot to handle she is.
She is the one. Yes, she is the only one.
Fully responsible for the day of stolen sex,
With someone that she barely knows,
But he pretends to love and care for her.
Capitalizing on her lust for things of the flesh.
She knows his loveless stance but is still in doubt.

If she doesn't care why should he care.
Delivered from a hell of sex starvation,
Into a paradise of sex orgy.
No one prays to the Maker for mercy,
In a moment caution was thrown out.
She throws herself at a man in abrogation of decency,
In an attempt at a catch-up growth,
The maturation clock is further set back.

In the trilogy of Stolen Love, Stolen Kiss, and Stolen Sex, what began as a causal relationship escalated predictably into casual sex. The attention-seeking and theatrical behavior of one participant captured the admiration of a young woman drawn to instant gratification, inevitably leading them to bed together.

As expected, the woman became adept at rationalizing her reckless behavior, often attributing it to unrelated issues. She grew hypersensitive to perceived abandonment whenever he was not present.

Can forgiveness and reconciliation alter her perspective, fostering better judgment and foresight? Let us withhold judgment.

He felt slighted and humbled, not merely by the act itself but by the surrounding circumstances—gossip, denial, manipulation, and more— from someone who should have known better. It is crucial to recognize that exploiting anyone, especially a woman, is inappropriate; guidance and protection should be offered instead. This poem serves as both a release and a step toward healing.

From Ear to Ear She Smiles

It's been so long and exasperating!
She waits to hear his baritone voice,
Utter the sweet words of romance,
The affirmation they are still together.
She knows he loves and cares for her,
But to what extent is it a jigsaw puzzle.
Now, it is raining, and the phone rings.
She grabs the handset, praying it is him.

Excitement overpowers precaution.
At her place of work, behind her desk,
she speaks loudly and heartily,
oblivious to curious, listening ears.
Not at all bothered by those around.
It's her midweek wish in fulfillment
That matters at the moment.
She smiles from ear to ear, overjoyed.

Script of their phone conversation

Once I know everything is well with you there—your health, job, and all that—I'll worry less about how long it takes to hear from you. I imagine you're enjoying the pleasant weather on your end. The cold wind blows intermittently here, so the sun isn't as scorching as it used to be. My job assignment in this part of the world is gradually coming to an end. Honestly, I'm missing home more than ever before, not because there's anything spectacular waiting for me there, but because I can plan more realistically and explore many opportunities, which means a lot to me.

Anyway, enough about me. Oh dear, you're a constant presence in my life. Your spirit always accompanies me, and I feel compelled by natural feelings to open up to you. Something about you has found a vulnerable spot in my heart, which now glows as I yearn for you. What can I say? Is it your uncommon beauty or your sincere nature? You are a rare find—a once-in-a-lifetime discovery. Your correspondence feels genuine, and your honesty shines through. You are the woman I would choose to partner with, given the chance.

Come Over

There wouldn't be much in it.
That's my life without you, entirely.
Amid people, I am solitary.
Though they are decent, great, achievers high,
From each one of them, I am disconnected.
Thus, alone I stand in this massive crowd.

I am thinking but not speaking;
come over and let us converse.
I am singing but without harmony;
come over and be my chorus.
I am alone on the dance floor;
come over and dance with me.

I am seeing but nothing captures my gaze;
come over and let me behold you.
I am fully clothed but feel exposed;
come over and cover me.
I am walking but seemingly aimless;
come over and be my companion.

Lovers miss each other for various reasons. Companionship is not about sexual intimacy. When friendship deepens to the extent of not being able to go on without each other, cohabitation may be all that is needed. That way, they can see, hear, feel, hold enough of each other, and grow on each other.

Her Rescue Mission

A self-described innocent student,
In the company of the wild ones,
Though he was before they were,
Streetwise and campus-smart.

By Providence, he sighted her—
A tiger on the prowl, he became,
And all else mattered no more;
The only song on his lips was her.

In his sleep and dreams, he saw her,
Got bowled by beauty and brain.
Courtship on campus, a big affair,
Marriage consummation next.

Concept of duality in reality—
Blessed is their union ever since.
He tags it her Rescue Mission,
A manifestation of blessings of Higher Power.

This poem highlights the story of two college classmates. The female was very reserved while the male was wild in social life. The male surrounded himself with equally spirited friends. One day, he crossed paths with a beautiful, reserved female student who caught his eye. As their interest in his other grew, his social life slowed down and he devoted full attention to her. They became inseparable on campus. The love affair culminated in marriage. They have been married for decades now and are still waxing strong in a union blessed with quality children.

Strings Attached

Loving is conditional, and rightly so.
Don't deceive yourself or anybody else.
There are strings attached to love:
His way of life is what you like.
His financial resources bowl you over,
His lifestyle impresses you,
The way he speaks captivates you,
His complexion gets you transfixed,
His mannerisms wow you totally,
His persona mesmerizes you.
That you are considering choosing him
Out of the whole lot makes him happy.
Be bold and truthful to tell him the price tag.
Nothing is for free that is good.
The burden of measuring up to your standard
Is much less than the pain of him losing out on you.

There might have been unconditional love in the years of yore. Not much of it in this millennium. There must be something dubbed a point of attraction in cash or kind. This point is different for different people. For some, it may be physical while others may become attracted to financial resources, fame, and power, especially in this generation of social media platforms where women practically advertise themselves by posing almost naked, revealing their curves to lure men to them. A lady told me she prefers a tall, thin man with tattoos. Another voiced her choice as a heavily bearded man with firm muscles so that she could squawk under his grips.

Physician Couple

When two medical doctors get married,
The exchange of marriage vows is a reenactment
Of the venerated Hippocratic Oath taking.
One is upheld at home and elsewhere;
The other in the work environment, and other places.
Both recited in mind instinctively every day,
And necessarily reflected in action and behavior,
Making the couple decent and reverent.

In the household of a physician couple,
Daily communication is in medical terminologies.
Love is expressed freely in daily doses PRN,
Affection is dished out as food TID, QID, or more.
Their neural connection is beyond medulla oblongata,
Affirming that in the recesses of their heart's four chambers
Resides each other's love—no tachycardia, no bradycardia—
Soul laid bare and foreseen by 20/20 vision OU.

The desire for you sits on my SA node in a peaceful rhythm;
Your affection is permanently in my cerebral cortex.
Thinking of you normalizes my blood pressure,
Pulsations in my arteries: good prognosis of endearment.
My vital signs of fondness for you are within normal range.
Being with you romantically is as passionately ordered;
We are destined to be together and procreate,
Have a fulfilled life of happiness and a rewarding career.

Abbreviations: PRN - as needed, TID - three times a day, QID - four times a day, OU - both eyes, SA – sinoatrial.

While the main focus of this poem is on physicians who marry each other, there are hints at other instances where individuals from other professions such as law, engineering, music, aviation, etc., marry each other. In such households, the language of communication often oozes with specialized jargon and abbreviations that only those within the same profession can fully grasp. Citing some examples, musical conductors convey practical performance instructions to their musicians through hand gestures, the movement of music sticks known as batons up, down, and sideways, eye contact, and facial expressions. Similarly, a musician couple might use terms like "forte" and "pianissimo" instead of "loud" and "very quiet." In the case of lawyers who are a couple, their conversations might be tinged with legal terminology whereby they may be referring to themselves as legal advocates in prima facie cases. They may be engrossed in issues related to male and female anatomical organs by using legal-sounding terms like "solicitor genitalia," "fallopian turpitude," and "vas deference."

Irresistible Pretty Little Girl

Many things in you, there,
that I don't see in other women.
So, the idea of an ideal woman
makes the imagination run wild,
more or so for a lonely man
whose heart beats in lovely rhythms.

You dwell in my heart, pretty tall woman of my desire,
thinking happily at last that I have found my soulmate.
Beautiful to look at and very pleasing to converse with.

Though friendship has many challenges, loneliness brings no joy.
Finding the behavior of another person friendly and obliging,
where nothing is in question but the desire to please and be
pleased,
making it susceptible to feminine lure in whose mercy I am.

Sunshine in the day, you wow the crowd
with spotless skin and elegant poise.
Sparkle in the evening, you glow and dazzle
with natural beauty in a curvilinear figure.

Moonlight in the night, you shine with affection.
Rainfall in due seasons, you nurture the greenery of love.
Armed with luminous smiles, you surely soften the mind,
deliberately warm the heart, and are irresistible.

---

*Praise-singing one's lover in a way shows to what degree the person is
adored and valued. The questions of what you see me, and why you like
me are adequately answered without being posed. The outpouring of
affection and level of appreciation shown are beyond measure.*

Lover Story in Poetry

Commendable is the way you stand firmly and readily
in support of your phenomenal soulmate,
anywhere we see you both together, the unity is expressed
at social functions, formal gatherings, and other places.
I dare say that you are the bedrock of the family's success,
reinforcing the saying 'beside (not behind) every successful man
There is a woman of substance and not just any woman.

An embodiment of elegance and modesty,
she ranks among the all-time accomplishers as a professional,
wife, and mother with a myriad of daily activities.
Sometimes we find love, at other times, love finds us.
She finds and is found by love and affection
in the competent hands of a true lover

A personable International Dentist of repute,
the blessed work of her hands ensures clients
have improved appearance and articulated speech.
Additionally, she makes the edentulous chews and smiles again.
Beautiful but conservative, Simple but stylish,
reserved but purposeful, caring but decisive,
She has an attractive personality and a compelling aura.

To remain strongly waxing as a couple in a fast-paced country
with busy practices, devotion to spouse and commitment to family
is not by chance or luck but a product of mutual decision, trust,
respect, maturity and confidence reposed in each other.
Thirty years of togetherness in these days of cash and carry
marriages is a fairy tale and highly commendable feat

Love like theirs is inspirational and is a template
for spiritual bonding and strong family foundation.
Her unconditional loyal love for hubby, and his for her
has profoundly stabilizing effects on their progress and
progression.
And has been the success they enjoy as a family unit as manifested
in their exceptionally brilliant children and rewarding careers.

They Did It

It all began in the city of the Institution when they put tags on each
other
"Is she the one, is he the one" This kind of quip is typical of lust
and infatuation
that rock-solidified into a blissful union.
Back then, the rigor of academics and barrages of in-course
assessments
could not prevent them from being romantically hanky-panky.

They successfully navigated and weathered the turbulence of
uncertainty
of campus love characterized by cynicism, heckling, jest, jab,
prying eyes,
loose lips and wagging tongues in the form of 'lover girl, lover boy
You couldn't be deterred because it has been rewritten
and affixed with the Divine Stamp Approval.

You and Only You

If I had to say "I do" all over again,
it would be to you and only you.
You are a loyal wife and a devoted mother,
a steadfast partner and an astute homemaker.

You are laser-focused on your intentions.
Very decisive in your actions.
You uphold moral obligations
and display ethical behaviour.

Sharp in deliberation and
resolute in willpower.
Humorous like a comedian
Yet devout like a prophetess.

You possess a warm endearment
and a heart full of love and care.
Permissive yet eagle-eyed
in overseeing our family dutifully and tirelessly.

Not Enough of You

We've been together for so long, and our feelings are mutual.
We live together, yet I always crave more of your presence.
We hug and cuddle, but I never feel close enough to you.
We communicate often, but I can't hear enough of your sweet
voice.

Like two sides of the same coin, we are truly are
inseparable since we were minted together.
Even being apart for a few hours each day feels too long
when we're not with each other.

Whenever I'm in your warm embrace,
I'm amorously restored and romantically rejuvenated.
The longing in my heart for you is ever rekindled,
and with you, I want to be anywhere and everywhere.

Navy Commander Soulmate

Living in full abundance of grace
Of the Almighty Lord in His glory.
Reward you deserve in full scoop
For all you are, to fellow humans,
Our nuclear and extended families.
My loyal wife and co-sojourner,
A dutiful and caring mother.
Exemplary and inspirational.

War Veteran Navy Commander:
Records impeccable, dignity intact.
Consummate nurse with a healing touch.
A resourceful and generous woman.
Morally upright, ethically driven to do right.

A rare gem that I am lucky to find,
No one else suits me but you alone.
Your loving arms for a warm embrace,
But for only you, no one else cares for me.

My soulmate, blessed am I to have you,
My loyal friend and reliable adviser.
You are the one with whom I feel complete,
In thought, action and behaviour.

She captivated him with her radiant beauty and his heart yearned for her the very first day he beheld her gorgeous self. Many decades later, he still finds her an irresistibly endearing wife whose love dwells permanently in his heart and whose affection resides deeply in his mind. A multi-tasking meticulous career woman, the joy she gives to him is immeasurable and the value she adds to his life is unquantifiable. With his imperfection, sometimes he wonders if he deserves her but then, he counts himself tremendously lucky and immensely blessed that she is his, and he will be forever in love with her.

Section Two

People and Events

They Dance to the Beats

Smooth, soothing, and absorbingly captivating!
Highlife music is at its entertainment best.
The saxophonists expertly press their instruments,
Slide the keys, and create melodies with mouthpieces.

Sounds with reverberating echoes resonantly fill the air.
Tremolo and vibrato played by a lead guitarist,
Accompanied by a bassist who connects notes
With linear harmony in the 7th to 10th positional play.

A combination of carefully laid out motives,
Infectious melodious licks and solo guitars are out of this universe.
The delightful percussionist in the rhythm section
Proves to be a spectacle to behold.
He energetically beats the taut goat skin
That covers the twin hollow woods called conga drums.

A video clip of a social event surfaced on social media a while ago. The setting was a nightclub in the 60s somewhere in Lagos, the then capital city of Nigeria. The song is titled Big Belle (belly) man's (sugar daddy) disadvantageous display over a younger rival in love with his one of his side chicks. This poem captures what I observed while watching the video clip.

The instrumentalists did their thing professionally sending the patrons to the dance floor.

The lead vocalist in a white shirt, spotting a rabbit-ear (bow) tie is launched into a musical trance all by himself in reckless abandon and he likes it and I like it for him. Certainly, the big-belly man who denies him access to his girlfriend's space at the appointment hour deserves all the mockery from the lyrically sarcastic musician with a booming voice. Having to come again tomorrow morning is no consolation for a lover who is already charged emotionally and full of excitement when all he cares to do is lay his hands on her, romantically speaking.

The couple in white dresses are impressive by the way they groove and gyrate with a touch of professionalism on the dance floor. Theirs is no ordinary display of footwork. They hold hands and affectionately look at each other in a way that effectively underlines unspoken words of endearment. The lady's moderately sized hips and butts are seductively oscillating in tandem with her restless but luring waistline held occasionally but gingerly by her pleased dance partner. And once or twice, she grabs him by the shoulder in a show of loving reciprocity that makes onlookers green with envy. Myself included. It was an entertaining show one can't watch it enough.

A Lady Wind Instrumentalist

Wind instrument players are skilled,
superimposing emotion on feeling.
The verses, chorus, and bridge of their songs
are simultaneously blown into the tube in ways
that let the listeners interpret what they hear,
according to how it appeals to them.

Rhythmically speaking,
wind instrument music appeals to me.
The young lady adeptly presses
her alto saxophone keys and blows
skillfully and commendably
into the instrument mouthpiece.

As its melody hits me where and how
I need to be musically hit,
lightening my mood and getting me
mentally stimulated and energized
so much that I want to ask the player
to lend me his talent for a while!

Professional musicians hold a unique position among people. The fans adore them. They speak the universal language that people understand. The melody compensates for the lyrics that you may not understand. The rhythm fills the space and the beats get you tapping your feet on the ground or better still making you hit the dance floor.

Female and male musicians are admired by those who love their music. The young artists should take time and learn from the experience of the older folks who got carried away by their admirers. They lost money and fell from grace. Drug habits, chain-smoking, gambling, and womanizing are all too common with musicians.

As fame and fortune come their way, many artists succumb to the allure of groupies that pose a persistent distraction. Many successful musicians find them challenging to resist.

With his distinctively groomed, luxuriant beard, neatly kept sideburns, detached mustache, ornamental wristband, and Afro-centric attire, he has certainly crafted a visually striking identity for himself. His wardrobe is now adorned with African-inspired clothing. It is a significant evolution in his style. I wish him a successful music career.

Keep in Touch Friends

Your address I have; I will write you.
On the way to your house I know, I will visit.
The rules we have, let's play the game.
Witty banter and friendly teasing.
No distance is long for me to go.
To check on you and say hello.
Day and night, I am available.
So strong, our friendship bond.

Simple things we do are priceless.
There for me, you are; here for you, I am.
Affiliation, socialization, interaction.
Lifelines they don't put up for sale.

Series of musical alphabets, scale they give.
Notes of different pitches, harmony they are.
Now that we have the space, time, and energy.
Let's sing in unison and dance together.

This lyrical poem complements the lyrics of the same title in the Millennial Poetry book published a few months ago. It was inspired by two instances: the retirement function of a co-worker and a good gesture accorded to me by my schoolmates who graduated four years below my class, all in recognition of my efforts and actions that positively impacted our school and old students' association.

Keeping in touch with those that touch our lives by their kind deeds, good working relations, words of encouragement, positive influence, and so on.

Associate and Socialize

On the east horizon, there is the morning sun.
It shines for you and me unconditionally,
Scorching it may be, but does us wonder.
Behold the cloud-laden condensed droplets —
Rain falls on all without discrimination,
Life sustained, vegetation included.

Here we are, virtually in a group as it were.
Common purpose in mind, everyone,
Neither written nor spoken in the main,
But camaraderie fostered in essence,
Expressed in many ways discernible,
Noted and acknowledged with gratitude.

Different backgrounds, cultures, and beliefs —
From whence come decent men and women.
Here, one we find in a re-enactment of
How we learned and lived together years ago.
Old friends we see and new ones we make,
To help and support where and when need be.

The past shaped for us the present,
With onward movement to the future.
The reality of the moment is unplanned
Can shift focus necessarily away
From what should have been all along.
Impossible it is for years to roll back.

We do know not what tomorrow will unfold.
Of what use are our words of sympathy
To those who have exited Mother Earth?
Show love, give warmth, and express care,
When we still have the breath of life
To see and appreciate kind gestures.
Free up now, friends and colleagues.
Life is a battle no one lives to vanquish.
People are already there where we're heading.
We won't be the first or last conquerors.

More to life and living than standing aloof.
Fellow Alumni! Let us associate and socialize.

Few decades after we left university, WhatsApp medium emerged thereby, allowing people to connect and reconnect virtually. My secondary school and university classmates were no exceptions. Foresighted individuals created alumni WhatsApp groups to interact socially as well as professionally.

As time went by, it was noticed that some members remained silent since the creation of the platform. They never participated in discussions of any nature or even offered congratulations on members' birthdays and other significant celebrations.

Somewhat curious, I made private calls to these inactive members and uncovered a range of reasons for their aloofness. Interestingly, the issues were similar, though not identical, in both the secondary school and university alumni groups.

Some felt inferior and intimidated by the achievements of the more vocal group members. Others were overwhelmed by the demands of their jobs. A notable number had unresolved issues from their university days that kept them distant from their peers. A few had no specific reasons for their silence. Many were caught up in the rat race, trying to match their colleagues' successes.

The frustration of not yet becoming professors lingered among the diligent ones and disheartened them. As for others, personal issues such as wretched marriages, convoluted love life, being single, having trouble with children, legal problems, and professional switches contributed to their disinterest. As such they are not interested in participating in discussions or attending events like reunions, fundraising, visits to former teachers, and social functions such as graduations and weddings of colleagues' children. Reflecting on these issues, I conceived this poem.

Reconnection

Now with each other, they are finally reconnected,
after years of being blown in different directions
by the strong winds of change and reorientation.
It was a ground-shaking, momentous occasion.

The exchange of pleasantries flowed seamlessly
into prolonged bonding and tight hugs.
They planted heavy pecks on the cheeks and sealed them
with effusive bursts of intimate gist and narrative reminiscence.

This is the story of a secondary school mother and school son who lost contact with each other. They reconnected after three decades of communication gap. It is common for close schoolmates to drift apart after graduation especially in the years before the advent of social media.

In his words:

I am finally reconnected with my adorable school mother after 45 years when winds of change blew us in different directions. It was a ground-shaking, momentous affair. Exchange of pleasantries flowed seamlessly into virtual tight hugs, prolonged heavy pecks on the cheeks, sealed with effusive bursts of intimate gist and narrative reminiscence.

Although she resides in a different city, our physical reunion will take place at a Resort. People will be cordially invited. Those not invited can still come but not with their hands swinging. They must walk with their food and drinks.

To those who didn't have a school mother or school father, school son or school daughter during their school days, being a member of the old students' association is a golden opportunity to have one.

The single, younger alumni can take things a step further by having old students' association members as husbands or wives.

To breathe life into the above wishful associative thinking, however, all members should make every effort to attend the forthcoming General Meeting in huge numbers. You are guaranteed to take something to cherish forever away from the meeting.

Needless to say, I thoroughly enjoyed my days at the school. I dabbled positively into anything a curious student would dabble in. I was blessed with a circle of friends who were (are) like siblings, teachers who were like biological parents, seniors who protected me, classmates with whom I freely interacted, and junior students who embraced me as a pal for course schoolmates with whom they had no inhibition to interface with.

Matrimonial Journey

The graceful bride is elegant.
The groom is handsome.
A delightful bride is dazzling.
A princely groom is gentlemanly.

Legally bound by marriage vows,
Willingly & solemnly exchanged,
Joyfully signed with kisses,
Hitherto witnessed & endorsed
By us all at home and abroad,
On the days gloriously appointed by the Lord.

Matrimonial sanctity prerequisite
For consolidating mutual feelings
Flowing in the hearts and minds
Of our children the equally yoked.

The intelligent, respectful, skillful,
Self-sufficient young adults,
Embarking on a marital journey,
Consensually planned by the pairs,
Now verily enraptured in unison,
Blissfully thence to parenthood locale.

This poem is dedicated to all the sons and daughters of my friends and colleagues who married before the publication of this poetry book. Since they live and work in various towns and cities across different countries and continents, attending some of the events in person was not always feasible, primarily due to time constraints. However, streaming the proceedings live on Zoom and YouTube made it easier for those who could not attend in person.

Socializing, dancing, eating, and sharing drinks are experiences that virtual attendance cannot replicate.

My Dear Cute Little Baby

I joyfully welcome you to this wonderful world.
Your grandmother is in an Alumni WhatsApp Group
That boasts of many Movers and Shakers.
Therefore, you are blessed with several
Rich, famous and influential godmothers, godfathers,
God uncles and 'god aunts,' among whom are
Professors, Specialists in various medical and allied health fields,
CEOs of National and International Conglomerates,
Top-rated Politicians, Government Ministers
Based at home and in various cities around the world.

Instinctively, I know you prefer breast milk to baby formula.
Good! Time flies, and babies grow big fast.
When you start learning kindergarten ABC phonics songs,
Remember, A is not for Apple but Àmàlà gbígbóná (hot cassava
flour meal)
And E is not for Elephant but Ẹgúsí (melon) soup.
Your given names suggest to me
That you won't be totally 'westernized.'
I foresee you as a patriotic citizen of Nigeria.
Wishing you the very best of what life has to offer.
Warm regards from a low-profile big uncle of yours.

---

*This is a poem for the grandbaby of a colleague in a College Alumni
WhatsApp Group. The grandparents are Nigerian. Her mother was born
in the USA. She is married to a Caucasian American. In this poem, she is
reminded of her maternal ancestral root. The food and culture play
significant roles in a child's life.*

Borderless Lady

I went to a mansion in Palm Beach, Florida,
Bearing a gift for you.
But was told you not too long ago left
For Victoria Island in Lagos, Nigeria.

Then I went there and learned that you were
On a jumbo jet flight to the United Kingdom.
In hot pursuit, I got to London only to be told
You just set sail on a yacht headed to the waters
Of Banana Island Resort in Doha, Qatar!

Living up to your name and standards
Of an accomplished lady.
With a borderless lifestyle,
The wherewithal of a Princess,
The humility of a commoner,
Down to earth, genuine, courteous, and sociable.

I know of a lady who holds citizenship in two countries and is a legal resident in two others. She struck it rich when the business she invested in became extraordinarily profitable in a short period. She bought foreign currencies and deposited the money in a fixed deposit account. A risk-taker by nature, her gamble paid off tremendously.

She invested in cryptocurrency early on, and a few years later, she reaped substantial profits from Bitcoin. Wisely, she converted some of her earnings into spendable currency and purchased two houses in an upscale area of the city. Confident that she is financially secure for life, she began managing her business enterprises remotely. With guaranteed daily earnings of five thousand dollars after tax, she enjoys the freedom to travel globally year-round.

Workaholic

You are married to your job.
It's hard to remember.
It's difficult to say
Whether you're married to a lady.
Work is good.
It brings forth wealth and fame, success and joy.
But find time to relax
With the one that you love.
If not, Mr. Workaholic,
Playboy will take your woman/wife.
He's kissing her, holding her.
He's hugging her, maybe loving her.
And she is falling for the boy.
He's stalking her, following her.
He's watching her, checking her.
And she is falling for the boy.
You are always on the go,
Every time on the gig.
Today you are in downtown.
Tomorrow you are in a suburban area.
The village you are off to, looking for work.
And on and on you keep going,
Not finding time to relax
At home with the one that you love.
Before you get home at night,
The poor lady is fast asleep,
Blanket all over her,
Hugging tight the pillow in your stead.

This is a cry for help from a woman whose husband is juggling one full-time job and two part-time jobs just to make ends meet. They have two school-age children who need to be fed, clothed, and sent to elementary school. They are often late with house rent, utility bills are overdue, and car loans and insurance premiums are in arrears. With mounting bills and financial pressure, staying at home to support his full-time housewife is not an option. Many men find themselves in similar situations. Financial strain is a major concern, and health challenges only add to the difficulty.

Love Life of a Neurotic

Torn between two professionals
Nay, unprofessional
Two playboys' heads deeply sunk in
Between the mammary glands of a flirting gullible
The same day at different hours
She dabbles in everything the senseless dabbles in
With righteous indignation
Attention-seeking theatrical display

Winning esteem and care
It is just a fair game in self-delusion
For no one loves an impostor
But only to be fooled, used, and discarded
She collapsed in a heap of uncertainty
With a loud thud audible to all and sundry
Unstable self-image and lack of self-worth
Are the early signs of a neurotic in love

Swept away on the dance floor of promiscuity
Easily won over by a substance-addicted
On sex performance-enhancing drugs
He only adds to the misery of a woman
With an insatiable appetite for drug and sex
Interspersed with a desire for financial gains
All characteristic of a night affair
In a mood of quick gratification of pleasure

Despite being unrelated to the themes of this poem, a tragic news story unfolded: a 22-year-old woman was fatally beaten by her cohabiting partner. After the brutal assault, the boyfriend, her assailant, shamelessly sought help from a neighbor to transport her to the hospital during the early hours of the morning. The woman's mother disclosed that her daughter endured an abusive relationship for more than a year. The man frequently assaulted her with a cutlass. At one point, the mother concealed her daughter at a secret location for a while, but the daughter eventually returned to him. During her final departure from the safe haven, she informed her mother that it was her decision to live her life as she saw fit.

Pleading with young women to heed their parents' advice, the mother urged them to leave abusive relationships. What has everyone baffled was why the young lady continued returning to the abusive man who consistently abused her physically. Adding to the puzzle was the fact that the woman had a supportive mother who was never tired of helping her but staying in an abusive relationship appealed to her even to the extent of enduring constant beating. There must have been something positive he offered that drew her back to him like a magnet. Some speculated that they could be addicted to drugs or engaged in risky behaviour and sexual acts.

Loneliness

Loneliness is a deserted road devoid of love traffic
It is tarred with solitude and shouldered with reclusiveness
Loneliness is a long race coordinated by hopelessness
It is sponsored by despairing and run by the dejected

It gets a glimpse of a companion as it winds down a river
Traversed by an emotional bridge built by the uncaring
Its hope is dashed as the river folks in many directions
To pathways of greatness not promised by what lays ahead

They all empty into a bigger river, mixing and flowing
Relishing in temporary hope of making impact
But quickly and unceremoniously they lose identification
As the bigger river empties into an ocean with them

Being alone and being lonely are two different situations.

Being alone relates more to a physical state when one stays by oneself in a deliberate act. People may voluntarily choose to remain alone without a negative feeling or emotionally disturbed. People use are alone in pursuit of relaxation moment for rest and retrospection. 's Being alone may be fostered by circumstances beyond one's control. One may be in a new environment where and when social connection is not yet established. Emotionally stability is a key element in being alone. Writers seek solitude for creativity.

Being lonely is finding one in a preferred situation or environment. It is characterized by inability to be in a desired love life and social relationship. One may be among people from who one is disconnected. The hurt of the past, lack of interest in forming a relationship, living a busy life, selfishness, ant-social tendencies etc., are factors contributing to being alone scenario. Left unattended to, being alone may lead to negative health issues exemplified by anxiety, depression, disturbed mental state and physical deterioration.

Graduation Party of a Friend's Daughter

In the meticulously landscaped backyard gardens
Was where friends gathered in the ambience of conviviality,
To celebrate the academic achievements of a friend's daughter.
We ate, drank, told stories, mingled, and danced the moment
away.

Old friends, and new ones converged in the atmosphere so
conducive
To indulge in feasting on delicacies of assorted varieties.
Absorbing music across all genres booming from speaker boxes,
In the acoustic background not too loud and not too soft.

Oh, among her peers she was outstanding throughout.
Consistently and commendably blazing through,
Making it to the Dean's List of Excellence in academics,
Shining brightly in extracurricular activities.

An all-rounder student, winning prizes is her habit.
In and out of the classroom, she excelled in performance.
Achieving her aims and objectives, her ambition was fulfilled.
At the undergraduate level, she's all set for graduate studies.

To your bright future, I join others in toasting.
Endless possibilities are ahead for you.
In this joyous moment for you and your proud parents,
Families and friends unite in saying congratulations to you.

I received an invitation to my friend's daughter's graduation party. I noted the date and accepted the invitation. No need to read the invitation in detail at that moment because I knew it was an event I had to attend once the heart continued to beat in regular rhythms and the body was in good condition health-wise.

I developed an interest in her academic journey since she was in high school. She consistently performed well at the University and made it to the Dean's list of high-achiever students in the year that my daughter graduated from medical school with distinction in general surgery. Her father and I exchanged congratulatory messages as happy, proud parents would do.

Her academic achievements included the Student Leader Award, Editor-in-Chief of the University of The University Newspaper, and Study Abroad placement which she did in Germany and she now speaks German fluently.

The Night of Gumbo and Jambalaya: The evening before the party we feasted on delicious gumbo and jambalaya. Gumbo is a New Orleans dish. Exotic wines, palm wines in bottles and kegs, and a variety of assorted drinks were in abundant supplies. Conviviality dragged on into late night. We returned to the hotel for restful sleep.

The Venue: Her fathers 'mansion has a series of lavishly decorated living and dining rooms. The ceiling is adorned with a magnificent chandelier. Breath-taking embellishments on the walls and expensive pieces of furniture speak of luxury and opulence.

A side attraction is the cellar which resembles a bustling winery, with rows of wine bottles neatly arranged on racks and barrels occupying both tables and floor space.

The backyard where the party was held is a vast expanse of meticulously landscaped gardens in which corners are tranquil ponds, occasionally disturbed by graceful koi fish gliding beneath. The mansion and its backyard form a harmonious sanctuary of beauty and tranquility, a place where the rewards of hard work in the past and present times converge in peaceful elegance.

The Graduation Party: Guests began arriving at the venue in the afternoon. I was among those who arrived early and we got into the business of eating appetizers and drinking liquid that came in various containers to wash the food treats down the gullets. We were soon joined by other guests at a designated table where we all co-mingled.

Food and Drink: Any named southwestern Nigerian dishes and delicacies were available. Four different caterers were hired to cater for the eating and drinking needs of the guests and they manned their sections dutifully and professionally. On-the-spot frying of puff-puff (deep fried dough) and crispy chin-chin, suya sprinkled with spices, and big pieces of roasted lamb were freely served. Pounded yam, amala, and fufu were served with *soup of your choice namely ẹgúsi, ẹfọ́ rírò (steamed vegetables), gbẹgìrì (bean soup) ewédú (jute leaf soup) laced with fried fish, fried meat, tender pieces of stockfish and so on. We ate and drank to our heart's content.*

Music: The DJ was top-notch. His musical selection cut across different genres. No matter your taste in music, there was something for you to listen to and to dance to. The girl's mother showcased her musical talent when she grabbed the mic and started to rap to the beat. It was so much fun and a pleasure listening to her voice.

The Guests: Attendees hailed from various parts of the USA and beyond, representing a diverse mix of ages, genders, marital statuses, and ethnicities which truly embody the spirit of celebration, diversity, and inclusivity.

Conclusion: The graduation party was a grand occasion and a gathering point for several old friends. Attending it in a lively atmosphere was an unforgettable experience filled with warmth and camaraderie. It was a fitting celebration of the academic achievements of a brilliant young lady adorned with accolades.

Here Comes the New School Principal

Student-to-Principal evolution at the same school!
What a history-making moment.
I congratulate you massively on this rare occurrence
Of teaching-to-administration metamorphosis.

You are now the big man on the dance floor.
Swing, twisting, bending, lock steps, spin, turn,
moonwalking, flipping, or floating, every move you make
will be keenly watched and commented upon
as an unwritten part of your Terms of Reference
in your new phase of a tour of education duty.

Luckily and far from being at ground zero,
you are familiar with the culture and traditions planted
in the four corners of our Alma mater and ingrained
in your psyche and nerve fibers over the years.

Your students are your first set of priority
and your tenure will be measured by your performance
in academics and extra-curricular activities.

It is no cheesecake nor a walk in the park mentoring
and monitoring students, evaluating the teaching
and non-teaching staff members, overseeing structures
and facilities and ringing fences around indiscipline
and anti-establishment tendencies are oftentimes propelled
or fuelled by youthful exuberance.

Guided by carefully considered projections,
good understanding of our Association and a logical conclusion,
my enunciation is that you will enjoy cooperation on all fronts.

Section Three

Village Life

I spent part of my early life in the village, where my father's farm estate was one of the largest in the area. Life was simple and people were adaptable. Both the old and young took part in clearing land and tilling the soil to plant crops. The harvest season was particularly busy. Cocoa was the most profitable cash crop at the time, followed by kola nuts and palm oil.

Farming is one of the oldest occupations. In the Abrahamic religions—Judaism, Christianity, and Islam—the holy books indicate that the first man and woman lived in a garden. Although no mention was made of their specific occupation, their descendants starting from Cain and Abel were engaged in rural farming and animal husbandry moving from place to place as itinerant shepherds.

COVID-19 pandemic lockdown caused certain measures to be instituted whereby, companies were closed down, commercial flights were suspended, and private and public institutions were shut down. Health facilities, garbage collection operations, pharmacies, and supermarkets were among the few essential service providers allowed to remain open. This underscores the importance of food and health and the critical role of healthcare institutions and farming in providing health care and the essentials that we rely on in our daily lives. It will do us good to invest in farming, whether through kitchen gardens, or larger-scale operations.

1. Living on the Farm
2. Feasting in the Farmstead
3. Village Bukataria (Restaurant)
4. Pollution-Free Village

Living on The Farm

Getting the hands dirty productively,
By tilling the land and planting crops.
Burn more calories in abs exercise,
Better than in the gym with costly equipment.
Roasted plantain: handy snacks,
Slightly salted nuts are a boon,
After a hard day's work and a dip,
In fresh, clean lake or river water.

Cocoa and kola nut plantations,
Chocolate, wine & beverages,
Corn, beans, and pumpkin fields,
Farmers market fresh produce,
Water dam irrigation everywhere,
No land is anymore arid anywhere,
Cash crops in rotation all year,
Abundant supplies of food for all.

Yam tubers stored in the barns,
Boiled and pounded as needed,
Cassava grated and fried as gari (farina),
Fermented and preserved as ogi (corn flour),
Fruits and mixed vegetables,
Fish ponds and animal pens,
Poultry, snail, and crab rearing,
Big smiles to commercial banks.

Living on the farm: best and the healthiest,
Environmentally friendly greenery,
Serene atmosphere all for free,
No Pizza, no Dunkin Donuts,
Breakfast the very ancient way,
Hot, thick cornmeal of porridge,
Yard fowl eggs poached in palm oil,
Herbal tea infusion in a calabash bowl.

Feasting in the Farmstead

Soaked in fetched stream water,
So tasty with slices of coconut.
No sugar is added, but goat milk.
Yellow or white gari (farina) in the noon,
Not a bad idea in tropical weather.
Pounded yam served with vegetable soup,
In which assorted bush meat drowned.
Dinner doesn't taste more delicious.

Birds sing, rodents out of burrows,
Terrestrial inhabitants in a huddle.
Aquatic creatures are all gleeful,
And so too are the amphibians.
Invited minimalists and naturalists,
Feted and joyful in the farmstead.
Original local wine, water by the barrels,
Palm Wine—yes, Schnapps and Dry Gin—not really.

---

*Here in this poem, I tried to reenact what it was like when I was young
and used to go to the farm to plant and harvest farm produce. On a good
hunting day, the traps set landed wild animals. We cooked and ate. We
dry cocoa beans, and processed oil palm nuts in a circular dugout earthen.
Boil yam in the bid drum with oil dreg called ikete was consumed with
pleasure.*

*This poem recalls the way of life in the village where people lived close to
nature. Yarm tubers were stored in the barns. Cassava was grated and
sun-dried and dried corn cobs were stored in sacks. No refined food. Fish
and bush meat were in abundance. The dry season brought with it,
communal activities whereby people helped one another to build mud
houses and dig wells and artificial ponds.*

Village Bukataria (Restaurant)

A type of visual imagery inspiring a few lines,
To capture how a poet feels.
Back to basic, a life of palpable pleasure,
In a seemingly low-budget, open-space,
In a palm frond enclosure with all the fresh air.
Pounded yam in banana leaf served,
With assorted meat in the 7-condiment stew,
And washed down with freshly tapped,
Frothing concentrated palm wine and sorghum brew.

There is a tent stored nearby to be quickly mounted,
In case of downpour of rainwater that may dilute,
Concentrated beverages with high alcohol contents.
Right there they eat away their worry and sorrow,
They feel good inside and it shows on their faces,
Making do with the little we have at our disposal,
A precursor of happiness and satisfaction measurement,
How contented we are when we live within our means,
In the suffusion in the context of our social bearing.

Overhead cost is supposed to be low comparatively,
And by extrapolation, the price per plate of food,
Should be easier on the budget than what is obtained,
In buffet or take-your-order types of restaurants.

Planks of timber for the bench, logs of bamboo wood for the table,
A farmstead owner is made green with envy,
An eating joint where organic food items are consumed gleefully,
A lady who agrees to a date with a man regularly,
In this traditional setting rendezvous, will be a keeper of man.
She is as good as a wife and is ready to trade her maiden name,
A ring on her finger is in order and should be placed there soonest.
Only you can make yourself happy in the setting of Village
Bukataria.

No cinema hall or movie house in the village. Village bukataria, the equivalent restaurant in towns and cities is where people, especially the young ones go, to buy meals and drinks to take away or dine in, the latter being the preference of the majority of those who patronize bukataria. Water and freshly tapped palm wine are the drinks mainly available. Wine and beer were occasionally available. On weekends when the place bustled with social activities were the times generator-powered electricity was turned on for all-night eating and drinking. Dancing took place on one side of the bukataria.

Pollution-Free Village

In the hot sun and rain, barefooted they walk,
Several miles to and from the village primary school.
It served five villages near one another.
Right there, people of the same tribe and ethnicity reside.

Oil lamp used to study, firewood for gas cooker,
Coal pot for iron pot, banana leaves as enamel plates.
Moonlight is their equivalent of a street light.
Pit latrine instead of a flush toilet.

The bathroom is made of dried palm fronds in the backyard.
Cultivating the land was their amusement.
Forest with wildlife passed for the zoological garden.
On the farm, they climb trees and pick fruits.

Hunting animals, digging soil to harvest yams,
Catching crabs in the swamps and fishing
With locally made nets and hooks.
Ultimate fun-filled pastime for the old young and old,
Primitive life they live in the village,
In a pollution-free environment, healthy, happy, and long they live.

The last time I visited my village was a few days before enrolling in the first year of secondary school. As the saying goes, 'You can take someone out of his village, but you can't take his village out of him. This is a saying that resonates deeply with me. Even today, my study room may not match expectations. It lacks tiles or a rug; making the floor somehow dust and I regularly wet it before sweeping it to keep dust at bay. It is only a simple wooden chair and table that I have inside. No wardrobe exists there for the few clothes I have there. They hang on a wire rope secured between nails at either end.

At my workplace and even at any high-rise building I go to, I steadfastly choose the stairs over the lift. These habits I inculcate and the choices I make reflect a lifestyle reminiscent of village life, serving as a constant reminder to stay humble and respectful. I am grateful for how far I've come and reached thus far. These practices reinforce the values instilled in me from my upbringing and humble beginning.

SECTION FOUR
FRIENDS AND COLLEAGUES

This section owes much to the WhatsApp groups of secondary school and university alumni that I belong to. These social platforms allow me to reconnect with classmates, old friends, and colleagues, enhancing my understanding of their true personalities. I celebrate their birthdays and other events by gifting them poems. The works included here are a result of these poetic exercises and some of my earlier writings from secondary school and university. With a few exceptions, this section does not include footnotes for each poem.

The poems here are inspired by the friendships I cherish with individuals from primary school, secondary school, and tertiary institutions. Their professions, personalities, and hobbies are reflected in the way they are described and praised. Although they are not named for privacy reasons, each person will easily recognize the poems meant for them through the descriptions.

Retirement, birthdays, job promotions, housewarmings, admissions into educational institutions, matriculations, graduations, and the birth of a baby are all significant events that are celebrated. Most of the poems in this section specifically address these occasions. Individuals and their unique qualities are recognized, and tributes are paid accordingly.

The most cherished gifts one can receive from well-wishers are not necessarily monetary. Recognition and heartfelt appreciation from co-workers, colleagues, and peers are equally valuable. Being praised, especially by appreciative members of one's household, workplace, community, and places of worship, serves as a powerful endorsement of one's worth and a testament to good character.

All the poems you will read below are based on reality—no fiction, imagination, or embellishments. As a result, the language is more prose-driven than traditionally poetic.

Pastoral Obligations

Not by coincidence that you have your footing
In the sphere of intercontinental evangelism.
You got called by Him, and in faith you obeyed.
You feed mankind not only with bread and butter,
But also with textual, expository, and devotional sermons
That indeed are nutrients for spiritual growth.

Tenaciously religious and churchly in pursuits,
Garments of worship you wear with pride.
Your voice of supplication is heard by the Lord,
Habitual in the offering of thanksgiving.
Your efforts in evangelical redemption of souls,
In fulfillment of pastoral obligations, are rewarded.

Empowered by the Holy Ghost at all times,
Fortified by prayers that work every day.
Strong in faith and unshaken in belief,
Gracefully and gloriously you are on a crusade
Until the Gospel is peacefully preached
Everywhere and anywhere around the world.

You teach and do right by the multitude
With the fervour of a crusader that you truly are
In mind-awakening and soul-winning ministration
That steers, men and women onto the right path.
In the fullness of time, the persevering believers
Shall live happily and eternally in the hereafter.

The Primordial Disc Jockey

Curating evergreen millennial tunes,
You spin discs to heal and entertain.
A passion you've nurtured
Since your teenage years.

Music and medicine,
A potent therapy, expertly blended
By the primordial Disk Jockey
To provide complete care.

For those who can't swallow pills
Or endure injections,
You offer healing rhythms
From your jukeboxes.

Music holds a special place in his heart. During college, he amassed a vast collection of both local and foreign music albums that were commercially released. Apart from his interests in sightseeing and photography, nothing compares to his passion for listening to and playing music. It's no surprise that he took on the role of our Disc Jockey at every social function during college. Now, as an alumnus, he remains the one who spins the discs for us during our reunion gatherings, keeping the music alive.

A High Achiever Anesthetist

Mountain of achievements, ocean of attainments.
Native intellectual, endowed with great wisdom.
Sensational bloke, a phenomenal human, and an eclectic thinker.
Knowledgeable in religious doctrine, creed, and gospel.

Broad smiles, infectious laughter, and a winsome grin.
Unambiguous in approach, transparent in dealings.
Humble guy, meticulous planner, flawless implementer.
Unblemished in reputation, distinguished in character.

Not alone in my adoration of you on this auspicious day,
I echo the sentiments and expressions of many colleagues.
Hold you in high regard we all do for your unique persona.
In millions of minds, souls, and hearts, you deservedly dwell.

A man with the longitude of compassion and latitude of affection.
So gentlemanly to offend, and so understanding to take offense.
Too nice to be forgotten, conspicuously present to be ignored.
High Achiever Anesthetist in the constant revolution of excellent
outputs.

You carefully and relentlessly search for solutions and resolutions.
Your innovative ways of simplifying complex subjects are
legendary.
No surprise your life is exemplary and you are such a success
story.
The bond of love you share with your family is guaranteed
unbreakable.

---

*Staying healthy and getting wealthy in obedient service to God for the
good of humanity is my prayer for you as you continue to live a life of
grace and gratitude into the distant future.*

Great International Dental Surgeon

No carious tooth,
No curious look,
No crooked teeth,
No dental implant.
Jaw wiring isn't that sexy,
But the asymmetry is fixed,
Much to the client's delight.
You are so unmatched
In what you know well
And at what you do best.
The edentulous smiles,
Once again and forever.
Praised be thy skillful hands,
Great International Dental Surgeon.

I Treasure You All

I feel very blessed
To have you as colleagues,
To be among you—
Decent men and women.

Certainly, I don't know
How things would have been
Without all of you
By my side.

With differences in beliefs,
Cultures, and backgrounds,
We are all here gathered
Surely for a purpose.

Let's do all that we can
To help one another,
To support and care
In every way.

I treasure all of you,
I appreciate your messages.
So much fun being together,
Blessing of the Lord unto everyone.

I wrote this to acknowledge the friends, colleagues, and acquaintances who have been part of my journey from childhood to the present. With some of you, I've shared unforgettable experiences that might have derailed our ambitions if we hadn't been there to support one another. Together, we've endured setbacks and celebrated successes at various stages of our lives.

This Is the Set to Beat

The Set folks are wonderful—
Certainly not debatable.
They are strongly united;
Yes, this is so obvious.
Members are cute and happy;
It clearly shows.
They are rich and generous—
We all know it.
Ladies are actively involved,
While the men are outnumbered.
It was a huge attendance;
The numbers speak for themselves.
Motivational and inspiring,
These alumni are.
On the General Leader Board,
They rank among the best.
On my unbiased scorecard,
This is the Set to beat.

This poem is an appreciation of an award given to me by my schoolmates who graduated four years after my class. It was in recognition and appreciation of my consistent meritorious service to our old students' association and our alma matter.

Award Acceptance Speech

It gives me the utmost pleasure to stand here before you adorable Ladies and dapper Gentlemen in the cohort of 1979/1984. I am enthused to associate with every one of you in this gathering of progressive alumni of our great institution 'Ahmadiyya, now Anwar-Ul-Islam Grammar School.'

When I joined the Old Students' Association WhatsApp forum in December 2017, it never for once crossed my mind that people of your sort would be noticing the sundry contributions I have been making on and off social media, in the upliftment of AGSOSA. For this act of recognition of me by you, I genuinely express my boundless gratitude to you fellow alumni for considering me worthy of deserving of an award. I view this award as a call for me to be more dedicated to alumni and other services of human nature. And I promise to get better at what I do so that you can present me with more awards!

I enjoyed my days as a student of our alma mater. And now, am having an extension of those gone-by days by being among you this moment of auspicious occasion of deliberation, reflection, and socialization. While at school, I benefitted from the loyal friendship of classmates, solid mentoring by teachers, and meaningful association with senior colleagues. Unequivocally, I am bold to tell you that, of all the institutions I have passed through to receive education and training, my secondary school has been the most impactful in my life.

As we ponder the way forward in our personal and group endeavors, there are bound to be challenges to be faced at various junctures of life journey. Let us not our spirit be dampened but instead, let us be strengthened by the obstacles. We must not lose sight of our goals until they are achieved. There are late bloomers among us. Remember that. So, as long as we are alive and living, nothing is unsurmountable. Every target is achievable. Unalterably am convinced; that we are only limited by our inaction.

In closing, my sincere admiration, unalloyed regards, and deepest respect are hereby conveyed to you all, from the Executive to the general membership of your enviable Organization. You shall all be honored many folds in return. I leave you with this lyrical poem below.

The Pulmonologist

"I can't breathe," he said,
Loud enough that we all heard.
Alas, pulmonologist you weren't there
In time to open his airways,
To expand his lungs somehow
With a needed breath of life.

By breath, we shall live;
By food, we shall grow.
Internationally trained,
Regionally established,
You are as important
As your area of expertise.

Multi-Faceted Career Woman

You wear many hats with grace and distinction,
At a time when religious commitments
Intersect with social responsibilities,
Each complements the other
In a multi-faceted career.
As a physician, you heal bodily organs;
As a pastor, you guide and uplift;
As a realtor, you provide a roof overhead;
As a group member, you play crucial roles;
As a motivational speaker, you inspire.

Cardiothoracic Surgeon

Destined for greatness, tailored for success,
Pragmatic and efficient, proven in skill,
With a fine touch and precision cut,
A scalpel with a healing power.
A lively spirit, fit as a fiddle,
An essential colleague, a truly esteemed alumnus,
When a Cardiothoracic Surgeon is on the case,
Heart and lung ailments retreat,
Leaving patients hale and hearty.

The Maxillofacial Surgeon Friend

Studious and sedulous,
Bookish and scientific,
Diligent and cerebral,
Erudite and scholarly.
Compassionate physician
And maxillofacial surgeon,
International lawyer,
Reliable friend and trusted colleague.

This poem is a celebration of a close friend whose lifelong dedication to his professional and personal growth is remarkably unparalleled. He has been academically recognized by and earned accolades from prestigious institutions across the countries in Africa, Europe and the United Kingdom, Australasia, the United States, and the West Indies.

Whatever project he sets his mind and eyes on, he pursues unwaveringly until the result is satisfactorily achieved. He balances his life so well that it fits into his schedule of extensive reading, frequent travel, and social interaction all of which he navigates with thoughtful considerations.

He enjoys a variety of activities—eating and drinking non-alcoholic beverages, sleeping and staying awake as needed, spending generously while also practicing frugality, and being either loud or quietly reserved depending on the context.

Despite his quirks, he is the epitome of kindness and support to his students. He delivers his teaching so well that the exam results favour them all.

With an impressive array of degrees—MBBS, BDS, FICDS, FRACS, FWACS, LLB, LLM, MSC, and PhD—he might just deserve a place in the Guinness Book of Records.

I often joke with him about his numerous qualifications, saying he'll soon surpass a thermometer in the number of degrees he holds. The real question will be whether they'll be measured in Celsius or Fahrenheit.

Simply Adorable

Simple adorable, you beat them all
On the global stage of career women.
Sculptured frame in smooth skin,
Beauty so pure and undiluted.
Attractive and strongly appealing,
Admiring gentlemen on the prowl,
Eager to pounce on a gorgeous one.
Despite this, you are happily married.

Godly and virtuous,
Author and motivator,
Colleague and friend,
Respected and loved.
Benevolent physician,
Community activist,
Great philanthropist,
Trusted fundraiser.

Maturity complements wisdom,
Conservatism counterbalances liberalism,
Gentility and exuberance juxtaposed.
Lifestyle of motivation,
Inspiring ways of accomplishment,
Socially attuned behavior patterns.

An individual so highly regarded,
A colleague very much respected,
That I have to relax my self-imposed gag order a little.
You refill my stylus with ink,
Making it mightier than ever before,
And whisking me away from intellectual inertia.

A Goodly Professor

Egg Head in life-long learning:
Decades of teaching,
A mountain of research papers,
Tons of peer-reviewed publications.
Much more are the why and how.
You have made it big in academics
And found pleasure and treasure
In academics and academia,

A repository of wisdom.
Spring of knowledge,
That many drink from.
Promontory of achievement.

Authority on contemporary issues,
Locally, regionally and internationally.
Good professor and great human being,
Impacting fellow humans positively.

A Brilliant Ophthalmic Surgeon

Rub on me your hands of affluence and wherewithal,
Gentle in manners but very powerful in deeds,
A tall man who towers above all trivialities,
A student genius, a blender of extracurricular activities,
And an erudite professional,
A man of might and means.
You work and dwell in the salubrious area of the city,
Possessing winsome smiles and enchanting attributes
Get you surrounded by a bevy of beautiful women
And a gender-mixed group of accomplished people.
Duly trained and certified, qualified,
Professionally evaluated and licensed,
Internationally assessed and validated,
Knowledgeable.
The glaucoma-afflicted can thread the needle,
The visually impaired boast of 20/20 vision,
Owing to the skill of a competent professional,
The Intercontinental Ophthalmic Surgeon.
The innovative Founder of Vision Clinic,
Delightful, soft-hearted employer of labour,
A blissfully contented, caring family man,
An emblem of everything that is blessed.
A towering leader with beneficial information,
The utility team player with a winning attitude,
A friend reputed for illuminating conversation,
A trendsetting colleague who radiates joy for all.

Appointed to Serve Humanity

A well-qualified individual with a caring heart,
Great mind replete with emotional intelligence.
You soar very high on the horizon,
With the ability and capability to do well that you possess.
In the lofty position you are accorded,
You are the best in this new adventure of service
To fellow humans with honesty and fairness,
A man of accountability and dignity.

A note sent to the appointee reads:

We are delighted and grateful to Allah for your remarkable achievements. Your recent appointment as Chairman of the State Service Commission comes as no surprise to us. We rejoice in your success and proudly celebrate your new role in this esteemed position.

On behalf of the entire membership of our organization, including current staff and students of our alma mater, I extend my heartfelt congratulations and best wishes for your new role.

With the State hosting one of the largest career civil services in the country, the task ahead of you is indeed significant. However, we have full confidence in your capable hands and are assured of your success as you give your best effort. To you, Sir, I say onward and upward.

Religious and Social

Many qualities we see in you,
That are lacking in many people.
Glamorous and angelic,
Yours is purely undiluted beauty.
Trendy in fashion and richly attired,
You dazzle and glow in a breathtaking body frame.

Tenaciously religious and unflinchingly adherent,
You are deservingly turbaned Iya Adinni Musulumi,
Empowered and fortified by the Holy Quran.
All adversaries are trampled upon and conquered,
Doing it the way of Prophet Muhammed (PBUH).
You flatten the hills and fill the valleys of obstruction.

From all of us members of our association,
Thanks and praises to Allah
On behalf of your radiant self
And gorgeous individuality.
In celebrating this birthday occasion
Of a social and religious lady.

A Good Alumna

Elegant in strides with the latest in vogue,
You are the epitome of sophistication.
Ageless body in spotless skin,
Evidence of good genetic inheritance.
Young at heart and mature in outlook,
The hallmark of goodness and graciousness.

Aglow with happiness each passing day,
Loved much more than imagined.
Working harder and surely doing well,
Appreciated more than can be described.
Attentive and in-depth in deliberation,
Precise and decisive in implementation.

For your natal day celebration, Madam,
Take my virtual hugs and well-wishes
As tokens of affection and gratitude
For being the alumna that you are.

Sensational Ophthalmologist

Duly trained and certified,
Professionally evaluated and licensed,
Internationally assessed and validated,
Sensational ophthalmologist of repute.

The glaucoma-afflicted can thread the needle,
The visually impaired boast of 20/20 vision,
Owing to the skill of a competent professional,
The Intercontinental Ophthalmic Surgeon.

The innovative Founder of The Eye Doctors,
Delightful, soft-hearted employer of labor,
A blissfully contented, caring family man,
An emblem of everything that is blessed.

A towering leader with beneficial information,
The utility team player with a winning attitude,
A friend reputed for illuminating conversation,
A trendsetting colleague who radiates joy for all.

Prayer and Atonement

In the river of wealth, we shall swim;
In the pool of prosperity, we shall bathe;
In homes of peace and love, we shall dwell;
In honesty and uprightness, we deal.

For our hard work, we shall be rewarded;
Integrity and moral rectitude are what we live by.

On top of our challenges, we shall be;
A very long and healthy life, we shall all live.

If slighted by me, know it's not the intention;
If offended by my words and deeds, forgive me.
To you, I say, let us continue beating the drums—
Play the rhythm and sing the melody of friendship.

A Differently Abled Colleague

Challenging life situations—
He triumphantly navigated.
Circumstantial causes—
He cheerfully championed.
Impactful deeds he did,
A fulfilled life lived.
He accomplished so much
In his uniquely storied life,
Much to the chagrin
Of many an able-bodied man.
He wisely and unselfishly
Bequeathed a professional legacy
Unto this and future generations,
So that he is forever memorialized.

A Phenomenal Pediatric Surgeon

Internationally trained,
Worldwide recognized,
A highly gifted all-rounder,
On the frontline of academia.
Professionally superb,
Fine touch, scalpel for finger,
Surgical precision attested
Others' dream is your reality.
Humble and admirable,
An individual so blessed,
A colleague so outstanding,
Special among the intelligentsia.
Certainly, the exalted status you enjoy
Is a function of your thoroughness
And monumental achievements over the years.
Keep basking in the glory of a successful career
And job satisfaction, hence into the distant future.

A Golfer Retires

You've comfortably sat atop a Golf
Championships leaderboards on tours,
Swinging clubs with under-par strokes every round,
Ranked high over decades of tournaments,
Sinking aces, eagles, and birdies until
Attaining the pinnacles as Captain and President.

Having decided to bow out gracefully,
With trophies and accolades, not bogeys,
Now "on par" with us amateurs and non-golfers,
It's all glory and celebration,
As you enjoy a well-deserved rest,
With occasional plays to stay fit and strong.

Sophisticated Lady

A prototypical example of brain and beauty:
Successful professional and dutiful mother,
and devoted wife and dedicated alumna.
A graceful and gracious woman propelled
By good attitude to the high altitude of exactitude
Of lofty executive position in our association.

Exciting to look at and inspirational to work with,
Highly respectful and reciprocally respected by all.
Admirable and admired, lovely and lovable,
An enchanting, mannerly, and glamorously classy lady
With alluring beauty indices that bedazzle the eyes —
First, before going for the jugular and entire body.

A sophisticated lady with endearing qualities,
A lady of scintillating, unadulterated beauty.
Mannerly interactive, respectfully friendly,
Provocatively sexy, adorably radiant.
Charmingly captivating, stunningly attractive,
Elegantly enthralling, irresistibly bedazzling.

Mesmerizingly resplendent
Are some of the descriptive words gleaned
Your attribute call card is left in my mind.
Mouth salivates, tongue protrudes and wags,
Eye pops out the lids, head turns sideways,
Feet levitate many inches above the ground.

Body swings in all directions in appreciation
Of your undiluted natural beauty.
Appreciative and well appreciated,
Working behind the scenes is undiluted fun.
My wishes for you are many but chief among them
Is longevity of life spent in pristine health condition.

The Accomplished Career Woman

Godly and virtuous,
Author and motivator,
Colleague and friend,
You are respected and admired.

Benevolent physician,
Community activist,
Great philanthropist,
You are a trusted fundraiser.

Beauty and big brains,
Duality of career success.
Calm, cute, and caring,
You are the tripod of attraction.

Benevolence overloaded,
Consistency elaborated—
Hallmarks of a kind-hearted soul.
You are the one lady philanthropist.

You are adorable and surpass them all
On the global stage of career women.
Sculpted frame in smooth skin,
Beauty is so pure and undiluted.

Attractive and strongly appealing,
Admiring gentlemen on the prowl,
Eager to pounce on the gorgeous one,
Yet dispirited, you are happily married.

SECTION FIVE

QUEST FOR PEACE

Decades ago, I participated in an essay competition on Nuclear Disarmament, sponsored by the International Physician for the Prevention of Nuclear War, the Organization that won the UNESCO Prize for Peace Education in 1984 and the Nobel Peace Prize in 1985. Headquartered in Boston United States, it was co-founded in 1980 by American Cardiologist Dr Bernard Lown, Russian Cardiologist Yevgeniy Chazov, and others.

I joined the organization and since then, I have been a peace advocate. Being a member allowed me to attend its World Conference, and visit its affiliate members' offices in Canada, Sweden, The United States of America, and so on. I wrote two songs dedicated to peace. The lyrics are included in this section.

Somebody will get harmed if someone gets armed.

There are millions of people starving in the world today while billions of dollars are spent on weapons of mass destruction production. If you give the hungry ones a choice, I suppose they will prefer bakes to bombs; shrimps to shrapnel; money to mourning, and grapes to graves.

Why are we up in arms when it is everybody's wish to stay alive?

War Lords are a dangerous species that endanger peace-makers with the sole motive of driving fellow humans into extinction.

At a dime a dozen, many people will not buy peace. However, if the cost of war is the annihilation of the present generation to ensure there is no future generation in certain parts of the world, the aggressor will make the bloody down payment to buy destruction.

Peace-makers will leave an indelible footprint of decency. Those waging war will not be remembered for their atrocity.

Peace accord elicits handshakes; bullets and gun-powder are the tokens when there is a lack of peace.

1. Appeal for Peace
2. Elite Propagandists
3. International War Criminals

Appeal for Peace

I on this planet of neutron emissions
Shall sleep and wake with a throbbing heart.
Large megaton bombs scare me silly.
My palms are small a shield
To ward off the scud and
International ballistic missiles.
So, I appeal for peace and
Global demilitarization
By the year 2000 and beyond.

Peace treaty belies social insecurity
When we run for nuclear armament
As we would an Olympic race.

In dilapidated structures hide can I,
The aftermath of radioactive fall out
That fills the space with fire- balls;
Replacing health for all with ailments

The faces look aggrieved
And blood runs cold
The eyes are brimful of tears
The mind beset with sorrow
On the account of mass destruction
Inflicted by dangerous weapons
Deliberately made by a man
And unfortunately for man.

Superpower America; do away with nuclear weapons,
All mighty Russia; help see to human safety,
Beloved China; forget atomic philosophy,
Beautiful France; abandon the nuclear race,
Ever Great Britain; Peace issues are at stake,
Biblical Israel; thou shall not kill,
Cultural India; show the World your love for movies,
Religious Pakistan; Allah abhors destruction,
All other aspiring nations; stay off the picture.

Elite Propagandists

Spines for wares; ribs for cutlery;
Skulls for mugs; torsos for tables,
The United Nations condemns
Their delicacies of blood meal

It tastes good says the devil
In his kingdom of mass graves,
Inscriptions on the monuments:
There lie the remains of the martyrs

They fell fighting in defense of
Territorial expansion and domination
Racial subjugation and ethnic cleansing
Political interest and economic opportunity
Tribal sentiment and social segregation
Cultural differences and religion affiliation

All in a setting of elitist propaganda
Championed by the avaricious.
May their souls rest in perfect peace as pick up
The pieces in all war-ravaged parts of the world

International War Criminals

You build pliers across the gulf to supply food and medicine,
To the battered and bruised population of the oppressed,
Living in an open prison in control of an instigator nation,
Carpet bomb the defenseless civilians confined there,

Hypocritical complicit in genocide you are,
A peaceful resolution to the conflict
Only on your lips for you wield veto power,
Block every conceivable resolution,
To formulate a peace pathway, you do.
Compassion none you show,
Credulity and morality authority but none you have.

Prolongation of agony is the game you play
and the world sees through you.
International war criminals perfect the act
of playing victims and you know it.

The killers are urged on in their macabre way
by your silence and inaction.
Using weapons you supply and ship to them
in the systematic extermination of a race.

Slowly but overtly carrying out ethnic cleansing
by all and checking those who can.
Ostensibly in the worn-out tactic of self-defense,
you sing the 'never again slogan.

Disproportionate Ratio in the unbalanced equation
of who is killing who in that region.
In the unjustifiable purist ascription of terrorism
and terrorists to another group.

SECTION SIX

MISCELLANY

The Human Mind is the Farthest Place

It is not the galaxy the solar system is part of that is the farthest;
The human mind is the most distant place that exists, as far as we
know.
The moon and stars can be measured in astronomical units;
There is no unit to measure the mind, the most hidden place where
secrets are held—
The safest safety box with no padlock and key and no code of
entry.
You can guess its contents but cannot read them accurately.
Body language is a clue to what is in the mind, but not at all times.
Action may be a better predictor, but only if it is taken as needed.
The one smiling at you may be deceptively dangerous and
unpredictable.
Don't judge anyone by the way they look and the words they utter.
You can be lured into innocently believing and wrongly
condemning people.
Applying caution to avoid being misled will serve all and sundry
in good stead.
You can predict the nature of animals by their behaviour patterns
towards you.
A friendly dog wags its tail; a ferocious canine barks you into
retreat.
A hungry lion roars and wears a killer look when it sights prey in
the wild.
Happy birds click their tongues, sing, and whistle as they perch on
tree branches.
You are sure to get stung if you disturb beehives, knowingly or
unknowingly.
We know dangerous animals by their nature and are guided
accordingly.
Physically close to you, but from you, their mind is far away.
The mind is a brewery where toxic or warm feelings are distilled.
Someone may seem friendly towards you, but loathsome they are.
A caring one you think he is, his mind is brimful with hatred.
A gadget to read the mind would be a bestseller of all time,
But then, our circle of friends would shrink and disappear.
Were the mind to be known by who wants it known,

You wouldn't be a guess in many people's homes.
You wouldn't reciprocate greetings from certain people.
You wouldn't touch the food and drink they offer to you.
You would hiss and frown at bad-minded people everywhere.
Your disappointment threshold would move from high to low.

In the Palms of My Hands

The continents have become a home;
The countries are the living rooms.
The towns and cities are the kitchens;
The villages are the living rooms.
We talk to whoever we want;
We see whoever we want to see,
Not moving one inch from where we are.
I attend meetings and conferences virtually;
I shop for anything I want anywhere
And get it delivered right to my doorstep.
I pay my bills online and on time;
I learn and teach outside of the classroom.
I socialize while staying within my home space;
I listen to music on the go online.
I watch movies without going to the theater.
Multitasking is made easy with a mobile phone.
A small gadget of immense value in my grasp,
The mobile phone is a technological wonder.
It places the world right in the palm of my hand,
Making globetrotting easy without traveling.

A Day Without My Cell Phone

It was fully charged and unplugged from its data cable.
I held it gingerly, ready to read messages and make a call,
When it suddenly slipped from my hand and landed softly
On the rug just a few centimetres below the bed where I lay.
Something unexpected happened.
The phone screen went blank—my first experience of its kind.
Subtle vibrations I could feel when the power button was pressed,
Yet it remained blank. Puzzled, I was desperate to get it turned on.
The laptop I turned on in search of guidelines for a solution.
In hope, I followed every guide, restarting a blank screen.
I tried everything, even watching many YouTube tutorials:
Bixby, power button, volume up simultaneously pressed.
The phone twitched as if it wanted to revive.
I stared intently for the familiar logo to appear, but nothing.
Many WhatsApp messages from family awaited my reply.
An important business call I was anticipating on a deal.
An election for a new EXCO of my old school, of which I was a
part,
Were all now relegated to email notifications.
Adrift, I felt as if I was excluded from all the world's affairs.
I was now made to realize how integral my cell phone is to my life.
My lifeline to stay connected was in sight but unreachable.
All phone outlets were closed, and no one was around to reach for
help.
Truly disconnected from everyone, I was left to contemplate
The absence of my cell phone, my convenient gadget of
communication.

Giving Back to Our Alma Mater

Thinking aloud about our alma mater, as good old students are wont to do,
Mother institution that perennially churns out fine medical graduates,
Voluntarily, they fan out globally for further training and better job opportunities.
Internationally qualified and certified, they become in high numbers.
The college inexplicably finds herself plagued by decades of shameless abandonment.
Her bosom was clothed in dilapidated structures that pass for antiquities,
Almost stripped of dignity befitting her good old self, but nothing she can do.
Her classrooms are hardly conducive to learning;
Laboratories are yearning for stock replenishment.
The cafeteria and buttery are out of operation.
Befallen by high yearly intakes but lacking requisite teaching facilities,
Her library is replete with obsolete and tattered old editions of books and journals,
While patronizing students, teachers, and researchers engage in dusting down.
Halls of residence are relegated to youth camps, nay glorified hamlets.
While hapless students are stuck in the ruts where rights become privileges,
Pictures of sorry sights assault the psyche of the bewildered stakeholders,
And collectively, they are dumbfounded by the gross pictures of what was once pristine—
Now boasting poorly ventilated seminar rooms, empty computer labs, and a long list of issues.
But beckoned by ingenuity, we are pulled together for a course in extrication.
Equally envisioned folks find themselves occupying leadership positions in earnest.

All have embarked on the mission possible, running the show with
the fervor of Crusaders,
Giving of their precious time in the onward march to resuscitate
and rehabilitate structures.
Appreciating members' contributions and applauding monetary
pledges,
Do we have to do all this? No. We are just bitten by the bug of the
humane.
In a setting of voluntarism, we heed the pleas and clarion calls to
give back,
Paying annual dues and donating generously for the common
good, we do.

College Days of Hardship

Siblings of the same parents,
We were considered to be,
Carried in the college womb, not for months,
But years of grueling academic journey.
Lecturers with peculiarities for parents,
Nongenetic siblings for classmates,
Rigorously tutored in the art of healing,
Self-doubting steeplechase questions,
Confidence-shaking long-case exams.
Lecture rooms undulating playgrounds,
Labs not so yo-yo amusement parks,
Ward rounds dizzying merry-go-rounds,
Intimidating theatre sessions,
Mandatory clinic attendance,
Teased with in-course test appetizers.
Hellish main meals are never palatable,
But forced-fed for skill and competence.
Now separated by the Atlantic, Pacific, and Indian Oceans,
But bound by the oath of common course,
Men of merit and mettle now we are—
Outstanding professionals in various specialties,
In the medical field and allied health professions.
Locally celebrated experts,
Internationally renowned technocrats,
The days of toiling and nights of sleeplessness were rewarded.

Dementia Unkind

The head is asleep.
The body is on autopilot.
Heading into a life ride of turbulence,
Waking up to reality uncertain.
Genetic predisposition delineated;
Several risk factors are well-known—
Denial or lack of awareness, or both,
Inaction by the knowledgeable,
Unavailability of requisite resources—
Contributors to dementia prevalence
In the elderly and the not-so-elderly,
Totalling 55 million people worldwide.
The brain is dysfunctional.
Other organs function sub-optimally.
The mind is a long-distance
Away from the nearest person
And not easily, if at all, readable.
Each day brings a new challenge
For the afflicted and caregivers.
The relatives are stretched so thin;
Resources dwindle, and patience runs out.
Hope fades for the illness so debilitating.
The community is deprived of citizens—
Hitherto productive and outstanding.
Physical agitation is unplanned;
Inappropriate sexual behavior,
Self-harm and harming others,
Yelling, swearing, spitting obscenities.
Aggressive behavior is unintentional—
Pacing up and down and wandering,
Disinhibition and lack of judgment,
No memory of irrationality,
Suspicion of people in the vicinity,
Accusations against close relatives.
Cognitive decline is progressive;
Functional impairment is chronic.
Lasting renewed hope—whence to be found?
In the acquisition of training and knowledge

Needed to cross boundaries and break barriers
To prevent and manage dementia of all causes—
Be it Alzheimer's disease or vascular types,
Frontotemporal or HIV-associated,
Or due to other causes, known and unknown.
Protecting people from brain health calamity,
Adding years to the quality of life and living,
The song and slogan for those positioned to do.

Friendship of Convenience

You remember me when you need me,
The hallmark of friendship of convenience.
When messages are sent, you need urgent replies;
Your communication channel is shut down.
Tongue-tied are you at my success stories,
You lack words to express congratulations.
You get busy habitually and never show up
When your presence is required in my space.
Excuses are always in abundant supply
When I desperately need a favour at your end.
Far from being reproachful, truly I am,
Be reminded of the many times I have bailed you out.

You Got a Good Bargain

Joyful expression with song and dance,
Generates so much goodwill for everybody
Whether religious or secular.

Let a big party swing here and keep it groovy till daybreak.
Faithful relationship, fructifying courtship
Displayed prominently campus social landscape.

You are both among the sophisticated student couples.
You got a good bargain with each other.
You are there to grow on each other.

SECTION SEVEN
PRAISE POEMS

This section presents brief poems celebrating birthdays, chieftaincy title conferment, award wins, recognitions, and promotions, honouring friends, family, public figures, secondary schoolmates, classmates, and colleagues. Although I originally planned to compile these poems into a chapbook, I chose instead to feature them in this section.

1. Foremost Ifa Priest (Babalawo)
2. For the Masses, Physician, Pastor
3. Ile-Oluji Chief, Witty Psychiatrist
4. A Wonderful Cardiologist
5. A Princess
6. A Junior Schoolmate
7. Titled Egbado Chief, Consultant Psychiatrist
8. Esteemed Association Treasurer
9. Occupational Medicine Physician
10. A Great Geologist
11. School Founding Father's Biological Son
12. A Retired Navy Captain
13. In the Holy Land
14. Royal Birthday
15. Consultant Radiologist International
16. Meticulous Obstetrician and Gynaecologist
17. Diligent International Vascular Surgeon
18. Professor Man of Culture
19. The Matrimonially Pampered Lady
20. Dear Older Brother
21. The Academic Professor
22. Physician, Realtor, Pastor
23. Psychiatrist, Politician, Chief Imam
24. Enterprising Occupational Medicine Physician
25. A Patriotic Retired Colonel
26. A Lively Osteopathic Physician
27. Benevolent Certified Public Accountant
28. Woman in Health Finalist
29. The Aesthetician Physician
30. The Philanthropist Physician
31. The People's Lawyer
32. Judo and Karate Juggernaut
33. Dimples the Pulmonologist
34. Scholar UNFP & RH Specialist Physician
35. Dr Love the Consultant Psychiatrist
36. Anointing Oil Pastor
37. Multi-talented Physiotherapist
38. The Selfless International Gastroenterologist
39. Uniquely Mellow

Foremost Ifa Priest (Babalawo)

Obeisance and veneration to the esteemed Chief Ifa Priest
on the glorious occasion of your nonagenarian birthday.
For over four decades, you have been the highly esteemed elder
The mouthpiece of all Ifa Priests worldwide (Àwíṣẹ Awo Àgbàyé).

A revered spiritual leader deeply versed in Ifa divination system,
You teach and practice the oracle in a manner that preserves rituals
and customs.

You are the foremost custodian of Yoruba culture, tradition, and
folklore.
You preach and live by truth, mutual respect, responsibility,
kindness:
Shaping the character of the acolytes in moral issues and ethical
dealings,
And adding value to people's lives in the home, community, town,
and city.

Guided by Ifa, the compendium of ancient Yoruba wisdom
You have illuminated our path by encompassing
The Yoruba history, medicine, drumming, music, dance,
and general way of life at home, social gatherings, and formal
events.

Through your guidance, we honour the legacy our ancestors
bestowed upon us,
By invoking and pouring libation for spiritual awakening.
Through these sacred practices, we absorb the lessons for our
enrichment
To be passed on to the young ones in this and the future
generations.

A kìí perí Akọni kí á má fi idà la ilẹ̀ gààràgà.
A verse from Odù Ifa Ọyẹkú-Ògúndá (Ọyẹkú on the right, Ògúndá on
the left) says:

Eta kankan Babalawo agbe
Ló dífá fún agbe
Wón ní ki o rúbọ
Ko le ba gbórí' gi d'ọjọ alẹ
Eta sasa Babalawo àlùko
Ló dífá fún aluko
Wón ní ki o rúbọ
Ko le ba gbórí' gi d'ọjọ alẹ
Bi agbe bá ké, àwọn ẹgbẹ rẹ á ké
Bi àlùkò bá ké, àwọn ẹgbẹ rẹ á gbà
Kí gbogbo wa ó d'àgbà d'arùgbó
Nínún ọlá, ìrọrùn àti àlàfíà
Àgbó, atọ, àṣúre Ìwòrìwòfún
Àṣẹ

Pastor, Physician, FOR THE MASSES

I joyfully congratulate you on your birthday occasion,
the superb orator known as "FOR THE MASSES."
You are a great debater with eloquent expression,
And a poet with flair, and an essayist with finesse.

You are deeply rooted in religion.
Your secular humanism is fine though
You are spiritually guided, communally minded,
You are philosophically grounded, and marvelously diplomatic.

One special man, marked by many evolutionary changes.
Former politician and mobilizer of the masses,
A creative writer and passionate discussant.

A dynamic colleague with multi-dimensional talents,
A distinguished radiologist and accomplished internist.
Celestial in spirituality and reverend in hierarchy,
Grounded in your terrestrial habitat,
you are a committed humanist in advocacy.

I assess your natural ability as sky-high,
describe your love for others as ocean-deep,
and consider your talent as immeasurably diverse.
My comrade on stage in extracurricular activities

We represented our different secondary schools
Debating and socializing in the megacity of Ibadan
Wishing you countless joyful events in the years ahead,
with continued happiness and good health.

Witty Psychiatrist

To the witty, wacky, and the intelligent
Wonderfully accomplished psychiatrist:
Your dedication and compassion
Mend broken hearts with grace.
Helping those with schizophrenia lead normal lives,
Turning mood swings into balance.

You skillfully navigate the complexities of the mind,
And bringing cheer to the depressed.
A distinguished individual, brilliant and transparent,
Master of witty banter and specialist in amusing jokes—
You're a true joy to have as a friend,
Always dependable when it matters most.

A Wonderful Cardiologist

Oh, the Competent Cardiologist,
Another reason to put pen to paper,
Celebrating your special day
With heartfelt words.

You, the consummate professional,
inspire curiosity and ignite passion,
Filling your heart with care and desire,
Nurturing your beautiful spouse with endless love and affection.
In a home blessed with the richness of life and living,
You and your partner share a bond that radiates warmth and joy.

A Princess

So very elegant with the latest in vogue,
An epitome of sophistication you are.
Ageless in spotless skin, fine body encased,
Good genetic inheritance is expressed.
Young at heart and with an outlook of maturity—
All in goodness and graciousness.
Each passing day sees you aglow in happiness,
Loved and cherished much more than imagined.
Working harder and doing well,
Appreciated more than can be described.
Attentive and practical in deliberation,
Precise and decisive in implementation.
For your birthday celebration, Madam,
Take my virtual hugs and well-wishes
As tokens of affection and gratitude
For being the person that you are—
The Crown Princess in our midst,
Majesty, the Queen in our Kingdom.

A Junior Schoolmate

Some people add indescribable values
To our lives that make them unforgettable.
You have been one such person ever since
Your longitude bisected my latitude.

One memorable afternoon, officially,
In less friendly junior and senior capacity,
We still joke and laugh about it in reflection,
Even though it's been decades now.

Since our common education pathway bifurcated,
Navigational technology compass ensures we are in touch.

A lady of cool honesty, genuineness, not vanity,
Reality, not fantasy, fullness, not abstract.
Strong rather than wishy-washy personality,
Your beauty goes beyond outward appearance.

It certainly has to do with class and charisma.
You are a combination of both characteristics—
Winsome smiles and has a congenial temperament.
The stars will continue to align for you favourably.

I raise a symbolic glass of exotic wine to celebrate
Your birthday virtually as I wish you the best in life.

Titled Egbado Chief, Consultant Psychiatrist

Born noble, raised nobly with honour,
Living a life of nobility and distinction
In the salubrious Staten Island, NY.
A friend of the Commoners,
Yet part of the League of Aristocrats,
World-acclaimed consultant psychiatrist.
Residency Program Director,
Chairman of the Department of Probity,
A complete gentleman of substance,
Loving husband, devoted Egbado father,
Reliable friend, esteemed alumnus,
The American dream is a reality.

Esteemed Association Treasurer

Delighted to write you a few sentences of acclamation in celebration
of your birthday occasion on this glorious day
the all-time habitually gentlemanly and highly accountable
Treasurer.
Some men are just tailor-made to live a life of grace and dignity.
Undoubtedly, you are one of such individuals.

Very efficient at managing cash flow,
we appreciate your timely financial reports,
methodical reconciliation of our earnings and savings
as reflected by your accurate record keeping.

Spoken and understood by all and sundry
In WASOBIA "owó, kúdí, ègo"
are words that make every Nigerian a polyglot.
And no one speaks the many languages we intuitively learn
on account of money better than you our honourable Treasurer,
the man of few words but plenty of decisive actions.

Occupational Medicine Physician Friend

Kindred with a heart of gold,
A rare find among men of propriety.
You wish nothing for others but success.
No wonder you continue to prosper on all fronts.

Quietly but consistently, you bring relief
To your Ilesa townsmen and women by stepping in,
Providing them with free borehole water,
And meeting their daily essential commodity need.

Good-natured, open-handed,
Fun-loving, bubbly personality.
Wishing you a splendid birthday celebration,
As you rock and roll in merriment.

Our Dear esteemed Friends and Colleagues joined me in congratulating my bosom friend, a distinguished Occupational Medicine Physician, on the occasion of his birthday. His demonstrated, dedicated commitment to our Alumni Association is admirably inspiring. We poured goodwill messages on his head and soaked his body with best wishes as he rightly deserves.

A Great Geologist

You basked in the limelight
Since the glorious school days
Being singled out among peers
Stamped with a badge of honour
Credited for fairness
Reputed for sound judgment
You served with pride and dignity

Towering and gentlemanly
Inner strength is very palpable
Outward calmness reassuring
Predictably unambiguous
Well-lettered and well read
Kind-hearted and very caring
Appreciably respected & admired

A giant of Senior Prefect who was so gentle in manner, strong in strides and powerful in deeds.

A senior colleague so cardinal, an elder so dignified and an alumnus so decent. You were undoubtedly held in high esteem. Furthermore, you were an individual so friendly, a character so refined, and a member of an Old Students Association so principled with high standards of decorum in excess.

The School Founder's Biological Son

Sired by one of the founding Fathers
of our secondary school,
You are a man of means and superior standing in the Society.
Chairman of a North West Local Government Area
And Chairman of Association social events.

Politically well-grounded and administratively skilful,
Yours is a life of glaring accomplishments and satisfaction.
Have a joyous occasion.

A Retired Navy Captain

President of our associations and other national associations
President of the Nigerian Association
A man whose name is synonymous with quality leadership
and high standards, he is soft-spoken but loud in clarity.

Gentle in look but powerful in deeds.
Remarkably foresighted and fantastically inspirational,
Our association is bound to remain progressive with you at
the helm
Have a magnificent moment on this day and always.

you are a man of nobility and superior standing in the Society.
Politically well-grounded and administratively skillful,
yours is a life of glaring accomplishments and satisfaction.

In the Holy Land

It is birthday celebration time as we honour
Our incomparable Al-Hajj (Dr.) who marks his birthday today
In Saudi Arabia where he is performing Hajj in the holiest cities
Of Mecca and Medina, and worshipping Allah
At the sacred site of the Kaaba and climbing Mount Arafat.

You uphold the Five Pillars of Islam as a devout Muslim
Recitation of Shahadah (faith in Allah)
Praying (Salat) five times daily
Giving charity (Zakat) to the poor and needy),
Fasting (Sawm) in the holy month of Ramadan
Performing Hajj (pilgrimage to Mecca).

By your words and deeds, you have cemented your faith
and attested to your belief in the tenets of Islamic Religion.
You are a selfless benevolent and benefactor individual.
The Merciful Allah will surely continue to bless
The work of your hands many-fold with desired outcomes.

Royal Birthday

Born into affluence and growing in influence,
you epitomize the ideal daughter and the cherished wife.
Your generous donations drive and support
the noble cause of our alma mater.

We congratulate you on two significant milestones:
the conferment of your chieftaincy title
and your royal birthday celebrations.
We wish you many more joyful events in the years ahead.

Consultant Radiologist International

The Accomplished Radiologist in service to humanity,
Standing tall you are in the House of the Lord,
Your presence is felt in social circles of friends,
Your heart beats kindness in people's lives.

An extraordinary man and a successful entrepreneur.
You are as concerned with the interest and welfare,
of others as much as self-interest and welfare.

A man of good intention and transparent bearing
whose helping hands are always extended to those in need,
Verily I say unto thee, your heart is surely in the right place.
And your good deeds known to many are kept
in the record book of relevance and reference.
Have a wholesome birthday celebration.

Meticulous Gynaecologist/Obstetrician

Very warm birthday greetings are sent your way across the ocean.
You are the one well-versed in the processes of conception and
gestation
that ultimately lead to the birth of a new life referred to as a new-
born baby,
whether through normal delivery, forceps of various types and
sizes,
even vacuum extraction, or necessarily by Caesarian section.

Your expertise and successful practice in the United Kingdom
make birthday celebrations possible in the lives of many.
As an obstetrician and gynecologist acclaimed locally,
regionally, and internationally,
I wish you memorable celebrations of this and many other kinds in
the years to come.

Diligent International Vascular Surgeon

From the four chambers of my heart that are nourished by
coronary arteries,
I sincerely extend birthday congratulations to the Vascular Surgeon
International
As the one with in-depth knowledge of the blood vessels and
whatever organs they supply,
my enunciation upon you is God's unwavering guidance and
protection
as you continue to think more clearly, focus more intensely, and
hold the scalpel more precisely.

In the Inner Circle of a Professional Society of the privileged few
and the great ones,
there you have landed with all pomp and circumstance.
Of all your many accomplishments, this one is especially
monumental
by any standard of measurement.

Following heavy scrutiny of your personal attributes and
professional conduct,
you were declared electable. There and then, you expectedly
emerged victorious.
Soul-deep congratulations to you the knowledgeable guy in the
areas
Where blood flows and lymph drains, grossly and microscopically
speaking.

Professor Man of Culture

Majestic as a King in a fiefdom.
University Bigwig in Academia
Heavily honoured multiple times
traditionally and academically.

On Professorial chair,
You are sitting pretty.
In Ekiti Chieftaincy regalia,
You are standing tall.
Humanity manifested.
Achievements personified.

Where culture and tradition
Cross the path with academia,
There you are gloriously sighted.
The stars align favourably.
You shine very brightly.
And you undoubtedly excel.

The Matrimonially Pampered Lady

The matrimonially pampered lady
you radiate affection
and the charm of a well-romanced lady.
Don't let your love grow cold;
You must keep it eternally warm.

You're blessed with blissful compatibility—
a key ingredient for marital stability
and a loving partnership.
Fortunate to be in the company of such luck, you're truly lucky.

From the depths of my heart
Comes warm greetings and best regards.
Whether in real-time or in reflection,
a friendly gesture never loses its value.
I know you'll appreciate it whenever
it comes your way.

Dear Older Brother

It gives me immense pleasure to celebrate with you
on this special occasion of your birthday.
Without exaggeration, having
an older sibling like you is truly rare.

Your foresight was the reason I have reached this far.
Your sacrifices paved the way for siblings after you.
Your caring nature lifted the family members.
Your insistence on self-sufficiency makes us independent.

We are grateful for your many accomplishments
and look forward to overcoming any challenges ahead.
My heartfelt prayer is for the Lord to grant you favour,
and a long life filled with prosperity and good health.

The Academic Professor

Readers Become Leaders
Lifelong learning and reading,
Decades of teaching,
A mountain of research papers,
Tons of peer-reviewed publications,
And many more reasons
You've excelled in academics
And made a significant mark in academia.
Valuable experiences gained with perseverance.
Strong determination and commitment.
Days and nights of mentoring and supervision.
Innumerable hours of Continuing Medical Education.
Fountains of knowledge,
Repository of wisdom,
Promontory of achievement,
You impart skill and expertise,
Finding both pleasure and treasure
In the rewarding pursuit of scholarship.

Physician, Realtor, Pastor

You wear many hats with grace and joy
You skillfully balance religious commitments
and social responsibilities,
with each complementing the other.

As a physician, you heal bodily organs.
As a pastor, you guide and uplift humanity.
As a realtor, you provide shelter.
As a group member, you play important roles.
As a motivational speaker, you inspire people
to live better and achieve more.

Psychiatrist, Politician, Chief Imam

You are a grassroots politician with a winning formula,
and you are well-known for your balanced perspective
and reputed for sound judgment.
Predictably unambiguous, you are a highly educated and well-
read man.

An internationally recognized, notable poet, and essayist,
you are a respected colleague and a beloved man of the people.
You are a devout Muslim and an Indigenous man,

Your calling card reflects an impressive biography
that includes roles as a physician, writer, farmer, and politician.
You sport sleek, well-oiled beards in respectful emulation of the
Holy Prophet Mohammed,
Thereby, distinguishing yourself as an Islamic scholar and devout
servant of Allah.

Enterprising Occupational Medicine Physician

Tall in height, broad in smiles;
proud Itsekiri indigene,
outstanding Nigerian citizen.
Loving husband, a wonderful father;

An outstanding Doctor of Philosophy,
Reputable Occupational Medicine Physician.

Notable FACOEM
Recipient of the Medical College Award
for meritorious alumni service
and quality representation.

German Wall of Efficiency,
effervescent high achiever.
Reliable guy and a trusted bloke,
an admired and respected friend.

A Patriotic Retired Colonel

A senior alumnus with a difference
Beloved elder of distinction,
A vocalist with a sonorous voice
Indomitable school ensemble leader.
A stand-out among peers
Greatly admired and respected.

Trench-wise and battle-ready,
A sharpshooter who is peace-loving,
Crack shot yet never an aggressor.
A well-decorated retired colonel,
An avowed loyal serviceman.
Unapologetic patriotic citizen.

Gentle in manner, genuine in character
Our alma mater's historical facts repository.

When you have a pleasant personality and are generous with your knowledge and intellectual properties, naturally you've carved out an extraordinary image of admiration for yourself. Consequently, you get the old and young to gravitate towards you without inhibition. You have unequivocally earned their respect and adulation. Furthermore, affection and love for you will reside permanently in their minds. The net result is the evolution of sustained cordial relationships.

The above is the case with the melodious voice school band leader, archivist, memory bank, battle-ready, war veteran, trench wise, crack shot, top gun, tactics master, reconnaissance aficionado, commissioned officer, genuine individual, demonstrably humble, gentlemanly and inimitably transcendent Colonel.

Standing at attention in veneration of the decorated military man, I loudly and excitedly say Happy Birthday to you Sir, with a footnote of best wishes today and always.

Lively Osteopathic Physician

What do you say to someone who knows so much?
What do you give to a man who has more than you?
How do you describe the path to success to someone who has
already traversed it?
These are the challenges when a heavyweight like you is on the
scene.

Aged wine connoisseur, surfing enthusiast, ping-pong aficionado,
serial marathon runner
A great sports enthusiast, sightseeing lover, and aerobic exercise
buff.
An evergreen music collector and a generous alumnus with a
pleasant personality,
A successful physician with a thriving practice.

Benevolent Certified Public Accountant

Over the past seven years, you have been the foremost supporter
of numerous projects undertaken by our association.
You generously fund them with six- and seven-figure donations.
Your contributions have provided vital relief
to members who rely heavily and regularly on your support.

You manage our association's transactions meticulously and with
accountability.
Diligently, you carry out various accounting duties and
responsibilities.
Our financial records you accurately and without charge.
We greatly appreciate your role as a dependable generous
benefactor
You are a celebrated hero for your timely and selfless
contributions.

Woman in Health Finalist

If what I see aligns with what others see,
then it is clear across the board,
that you are a winner on all counts.

You are counted among the intelligentsia
and intercontinental professional women.
You are a consistent high achiever.

The benevolent ladies, your persistent advocacy,
collectively contributes to making life more liveable.

The poet's stylus is refreshed with ink that flows like a river,
ready to express heartfelt best wishes in celebrating
the rare achievement of a gracefully alluring lady.

We are delighted and excited about your accomplishments
and wish you the very best in your next adventure.

The Aesthetician Physician

We are all really enthralled
and thoroughly impressed
by the glamorous physician aesthetician.

Her alluring beauty dazzles the eyes
and captivates the heart,
leaving a lasting impression.

With a spotless ebony complexion
and a well-sculpted frame, she enchants
with disarming smiles and elegance.

The Philanthropist Physician

Beauty and brilliance, you embody the duality of career success with grace.
Calm, cute, and caring, you are a tripod of attraction.
You are overflowing with benevolence and consistency in your kindness,
The hallmark of a compassionate philanthropist and physician.

Unparalleled in beauty, you shine on the global stage of career women.
With a sensuous body frame and smooth skin,
your pure and undiluted beauty is strongly appealing.
Admiring men may take note, but you are happily married and content.

Godly and virtuous, you are an author and motivator.
A colleague and friend, you are respected and loved.
As a benevolent physician, community activist, great philanthropist,
You continue to inspire and uplift those around you.

The People's Lawyer

You are the freedom fighter lawyer who wins cases,
You outwit opponents with your deep legal knowledge.
Judges and Magistrates respect your commanding presence,
And clients trust you implicitly, mutual trust is the watchword.
For you, every case is winnable.
You are the voice for the voiceless,
You are the hope for the defenceless.
Your countless pro bono cases are record-high,
And pay-after-the-verdict policy endears you to all,
Making you the undisputed People's Lawyer.

Judo and Karate Juggernaut

Pain and Spine Consultant
Aligning lordosis and correcting,
compressed nerves from head to toes,
Expertly and permanently.
This you do for a living.

Martial Arts Aficionado
Immense strength in quietude,
Few words, yet action-packed.
A harmless Karate Grandmaster.

Dimples the Pulmonologist

Yes, you must breathe!
Inhale and exhale, slowly or fast.
Water and food can wait,
Singing and dancing can wait,
Love and sex can wait,
Everything else can be put on hold,
But not the air we take in.
Yes, we must all breathe!
Affectionately known as Dimples,
A specialist in pulmonology,
Well-trained and duly certified.
Honoured and recognized.

You bring life to the breathless
Through non-invasive or invasive,
Positive or negative,
Pressure ventilation.

Scholar UNFPA & RH Specialist Physician

Great and accomplished,
The intellectual that you are,
Looking sharp and youthful,
Your love for soccer shines through.

Dressed to match the global mood,
With the World Cup in full swing,
You bear a striking resemblance
To FIFA field officials,
More like a referee,
Assuring players of fairness.
Assuring colleagues of comradery.
Assuring UNFPA of accountability.

UNFPA - United Nations Fund for Population Activities

RH - Reproductive Health

Doctor Love the Consultant Psychiatrist

Dr Love, the ever-compassionate psychiatrist,
You display discernment to the fullest, always.
A distinguished alumnus with a heart full of love and affection,
Your maturity complements your wisdom,
Conservatism in you balances liberalism,
Your gentility juxtaposed with exuberance.
A religious psychiatrist whose lifestyle motivates.
Your quietude amuses fellow professional colleagues.
You are recognized and appreciated for your charitable work.
Your accomplishments inspire people worldwide.
You brim with tremendous knowledge and wisdom.
Tagging you with any title is simply a way to bid boredom
goodbye.

Anointing Oil Pastor

Important and enviable titles,
Earned through calling and true love.
Rewarded by hard work and prayer that works like magic.
Lovely, adorable, and fashionable,
An international lady of great achievements.
In obedience, you worship your Lord.
With humility, you serve humanity.
May you receive more anointing and deliverance,
With holy water and olive oil.
May your congregation expand,
And may tithes and offerings increase exponentially.

Multi-talented Physiotherapist

You are the physiotherapist with a deft touch.
Smooth palms and skillful fingers
They work magic on sprained muscles,
Keep ligaments and bones in alignment,
And restore normal posture to stiff joints.
Furthermore, you showcase a natural gift,
Effortlessly and flawlessly.
You guide people to victory through sermons.
You entertain people socially with professional dance moves
By moonwalking, stretching, bending,
Even gliding and levitating through the air.

The Selfless International Gastroenterologist

Your many good deeds are documented for posterity.
You generously support your alma mater
both financially and otherwise.
The knowledge you impart is deeply absorbed,
And the skills you transfer empower those you reach.
Reasonable and respectable you are known to be.
The decent and dignified man you are.
Your life is exemplary and impactful,
And your methods of approach are meticulous.
A prominent community leader,
You are a custodian of culture and tradition.

Uniquely Mellow

The continentally exposed and strategically poised,
Globally experienced and widely knowledgeable,
Guided by social navigation tools,
You are a man of exceptional attributes.
Born to excel, you are youthful in spirit,
A notable philanthropist, you are resourceful providence,
Transparently genuine and well-meaning,
a man with an aura of goodwill.
What a personality—uniquely mellow,
Conspicuously seen and loudly heard,
Where productivity is bisected by efficiency.

Acknowledgments

My daughter, Dr Bibitayo made significant contributions to this project in various ways. The desire to keep my son creatively motivated through writing was incredibly helpful. PHO Michelle Titus read some of the poems and provided invaluable feedback. I am grateful to all the friends, colleagues, acquaintances, and co-workers, as well as the many people I met both at home and abroad. Their diverse personalities and perspectives offered rich literary insights. I owe a great deal of appreciation to Ms. Kristy Christopher for designing the front cover and to Ms. Kristina Levshits for her dedication to the project.